Terms for Or

KENNETH BURKE

Terms for Order

EDITED BY

STANLEY EDGAR HYMAN

WITH THE ASSISTANCE OF

BARBARA KARMILLER

INDIANA UNIVERSITY PRESS

BLOOMINGTON

68,770

Contents

Introduction

As a systematic critic, Kenneth Burke is unique in our time, and his ambitiousness challenges Aristotle. He has developed the concepts of *form as the psychology of the audience,* of *symbolic action* for the poem-poet relation and *rhetoric* for the poem-audience relation, then of *dramatism* and the *pentad,* finally of *logology* and *the hierarchical principle, entelechy* and *the principle of composition.* At the same time he has exemplified these systems and structurings in dramatistic fiction, rhetorical poems, entelechial aphorisms and logological orations. In changing his terms ceaselessly while his preoccupations remain constant, Burke resembles Picasso; like Picasso, Burke will probably seem to a later age to have been a syndicate.

Our aim in this sampling of Burke's books and articles is to introduce his work to a wider circle of readers; not the thousands familiar with his books but the hundreds of thousands familiar with his ideas only in dilute and popularized form. Such a sampling can be successful only insofar as it sends its readers to the books themselves. That little gem, "The Range of Piety," is one of many such gems in *Permanence and Change;* the fascinating chart in "Tautological Cycle of Terms for 'Order' " is a graphic evidence of the intellectual complexity of *The Rhetoric of Religion.*

We have tried in this sampling to represent all of Burke's variety: fiction, poetry, and criticism both theoretical and practical, generalized and technical, symbolical and rhetorical. All of his books are represented except the two volumes on Motives, which are freshly available in paperback and are in any case difficult to represent in excerpt. The selections range in length from short lyric poems to Burke's long brilliant demonstration of "indexing," "Fact, Inference, and Proof in the Analysis of Literary Symbolism," and they include material not previously available in book form.

Burke has taken no part in the selection or cutting, which are entirely our responsibility. He kindly made a few suggestions, which are here gratefully acknowledged. The order is chronological, by the date of first publication. A second volume, *Perspectives by Incongruity,* offers a similar sampling of Burke's less systematic writing.

S.E.H.

B.K.

North Bennington,
Vermont

Terms for Order

The Book of Yul
(1922)

Part One

While waiting, two men carried on a conversation that flapped and fluttered like an old newspaper. And a third was silent. Finally, the conversation gained in intensity, culminating in some disagreeable figure or image. Whereat, the third man rose and left the room. With us following, for it is he who conceived of Yul and the eleventh city. Thus:

Three men in a room, towards night. Two of them sat in the cold, sprawled somewhat, and with their overcoats on. The third was huddled in a Morris chair, knees up to his chin, looking down over his toes at the vague carpet. "Do you think she will come?" one of the other two asked. He swallowed, and noticed that his throat was getting sore. For a while they shifted slightly, in silence. (As the room grew darker, no one had moved to light the lamps.) The sounds outside came in dampened by the snow.

"We should have started a fire when we first got here," the first man said, yawning. "If we're going to wait around here we might as well be comfortable."

"Too late now, she'll be along any minute."

The man hunched up in the Morris chair sniffled three or four times, and then blew his nose. "Ah, what a bitter world!" one of the others laughed. "Look, the poor devil had to move."
. . . A heavy clock, in another room somewhere, or upstairs, or in the hall, sunk seven strokes into the room. Outside an automobile stalled. They heard the scraping of the self-starter several times before the motor began working again. Then the car jerked ahead; then stalled. After a few minutes, however, the motor thumped with a solid regularity, and the car passed on down the street. Out of the high windows the snow could be seen falling diagonally across a street lamp.

"This waiting outside the gates of Heaven is cold business."

"Why in the name of God do you call it the gates of Heaven?"

Somebody could be heard walking. Thump, thump, THUMP louder . . . then THUMP, THUMP, thump fainter. "Probably the people in the next house." Listening intently, they could even catch a grumble of voices. Off up there, on the other side of the wall somewhere, people were no doubt sitting around talking, before a big fire, in a room full of light, eating, or maybe drinking something strong. Like those conceptions of perfect luxury which are inserted in the upper right-hand corner, the rest of the picture being devoted to a boy in rags, starving to death in a snowy alley.

A wind caught in the chimney in such a way as to disturb the burnt rubbish in the grate. The smell of rotten apples blew out into the room. Two girls passed outside, laughing, and hurrying with short, sharp steps. The man who had swallowed a little while ago brought up some saliva and swallowed again, to test his throat; the glands were distinctly swollen. He shot his cigarette into the dead grate; after a few moments, however, he lighted another. He said, "Damn this place for a tomb." A pause; then he continued, "When I stay very long in a place like this I always think, what if I were trapped in? . . . When I was a boy, I saw a crow early one spring standing bolt upright in a tree. I went closer, and he didn't fly. Then I saw that his foot had been caught in a fox trap. He flew to this tree, where the chain got caught in one of the branches. So he had been there during the winter, exposed to the cold and without food; and when he died, the trap weighted him so that he stood up as chestily as the healthiest crow you ever saw. . . . When I wait in a place like this, I can't help thinking of dying that way. Can't you imagine us all sitting here in this darkness, dead, you holding a pipe, and me like this, and him over there in the corner all hunched up!" At this point, the man in the Morris chair arose, left the room, and could be heard immediately afterwards going down the stone stairs to the street.

The snow was falling now in thick wet gobs. Before he had gone fifty feet it was clinging to the fuzz of his woolen coat. Big banks of cleanliness had been stacked up. The lights of the store windows lay distinctly across the pavements. In that arc light, in the carbon, in one molecule of the carbon, maybe, there was a little world, with planets and stars, and an infinite sky, and things living on some of the planets, and things living on those things. Some day some big hand would want our universe for an arc light, and crunch, away it would go. "In one little corner beyond the stars, a world glowing up there all by itself, not crowded in the way ours is . . ." God, what a night! He listened unconsciously to the different scrapings of the shovels.

He started to turn into the subway, but did not do so, since an elation was on him. Instead, he went into the park, and stamped about in the heavy snow, even walked across one of the ponds, in fact. A gust of wind hit him strong enough for him to rise up against it, and yell into the teeth of it. Then he swung his arms, and charged an embankment. When he reached the top, he looked about him, a half mile across the park to the lights of the apartments along the edge. The wind dropped away; he was almost hot after his exertion. He opened his coat and laughed a stage laugh. Then he chanted, *"Sic erat in principio, et nunc, et semper, et in saecula saeculorum, amen.* And the wind, appearing before me, spook, speek, spike, spuck, SPAKE, 'Behold the eleventh citee.' And I, answering unto the wind, spook, speek, spike, spuck, SPAYACHE, 'Verily, verily, do I behold the eleventh citee,' for there are ten others buried beneath it. Gloria!"

And then continuing to singsong the *Sic erat,* his mind wandered off to elaborate the eleventh city. "It is in the bottom of the sea," he thought, "and lived in by extremely cultivated fishes." But I happen to know that it is not at the bottom of the sea; or that it is not even near the sea. But it stands, bulky and dead, in the middle of a plain, silhouetted against the sky, and cold.

It is granite. Even the beds on which the people sleep are granite slabs, built in square holes carved out of the walls. For people live in this eleventh city: quiet, grey-eyed people,

who slip about the stone streets, and in and out of the oblong
holes which serve as doors. But the under cities are filled with
corpses, lying in rows, perfectly preserved, and without smell.
The streets are long straight lines, and other long straight lines
drawn perpendicular to these; the same is consistently true of
the architecture.

And there was a traveler in this city, by the name of Yul.
Looking ahead at the end of the widest street, he saw a break
in the two walls of granite, and went towards it. It was a stairway, he found. Broad stairs, the width of a palace in his own
country, led down to a platform, then down to a platform, and
so on down and down to platforms. All this was lit with a uniform incandescence. While at the base of the stairs there stood
two granite lampposts, of no great size, but which he could
distinguish as clearly as though they were immediately in front
of him.

But Yul did not descend these stairs.

Part Two

Yul found the system of transit which had been evolved here
of great ingenuity. It was composed of sixteen parallel tracks,
or rather, endless platforms, which moved continually. These
platforms were provided with benches, pavements, empty
rooms, and the like. Now, as Yul stepped toward the south,
he noticed that each platform moved slightly faster than the
one to the north of it; and although the change from platform
to platform was not abrupt, by the time Yul had reached the
fifteenth platform to the south he was speeding enormously.
The sixteenth platform, however, was entirely different from
the fifteen preceding. To begin with, he found that it could
not be boarded at any point, as with the other platforms. In
front of him there moved a stone wall; occasionally, behind this
wall he heard a roar, as of something which approached and
retreated. And Yul, noticing that a group of grey-gowned

figures had stopped near him on the fifteenth platform and seemed to be waiting, waited as well.

Within a short time he saw a tower approaching on the sixteenth platform. It advanced evenly, floated towards them, growing gradually above them as it came. When it was only a short ways off, he also noticed that there was a break in the stone wall at this point, and that some of the figures farther down the platform were already entering there. In due time it reached him, and he stepped under the square stone arch on to the sixteenth platform. Everything was quite different here. Instead of the stone benches, pavements, kiosks, there was nothing but this lonely tower and a straight steel track that blurred away to the east and west. Like the others, he entered the tower, and found it a sort of rest room or waiting room.

Finally, above the grinding of the platforms, a far-off whirr was heard. The grey-clad figures left the tower, Yul thinking it best to follow. A line of cars shot up to the tower and stopped. Yul followed his companions into one of the cars, and they sped along the sixteenth platform. Yul sank into a stupor from this accumulation of speeds, partaking of nothing but a bitter, burning liquid which was brought to him at intervals. After another two days, Yul tired of the cars, and descended at one of the towers. Then he crossed the fifteen other platforms to the north, and found, when he stepped off the last of them, that he had returned almost to the starting point.*

He came to the wide street again, and entered one of the oblong cuts in the stone which served as doorways. Inside, there were winding stairs, lit with the same unvarying incandescence that he had noticed on the stairs leading down to the buried cities. Yul wound slowly upwards, his steps slapping back at him in a confusion of echoes. The stairs curved into a room; a large, square room, empty except for a tablet on one of the walls and a bench placed before this tablet. Yul, who could not read the tablet, noticed the firmness of the characters,

* He had circled only once about the city in all this time, and that in spite of the enormous velocity with which he had been traveling; which facts, it is hoped, will tend to show the vastness of the eleventh city, and of the ten cities buried beneath it.

and passed on into the next room. This room, too, was large and square and empty. But there was a window hewn out in one wall, oblong like the doors in the street, except that it was lying on one of the longer sides. From this window Yul could see across the plain to the even, cold horizon. It was in still another room, the third, that Yul voided.

Yul then came down from this place into the street, and walked along until he came to a larger granite entrance than was usual. He entered, finding himself beneath a balcony. He walked farther and saw a floor of white marble, dipping in a slow curve toward a stage or altar in the distance. Yul fell upon his knees and wept, this quiet curve was so soothing to him. Looking above him, he saw that here, too, there were curves; the walls reaching up thin arms of broken arches; a ceiling behind shadows, and vaulted; and thick wooden beams that worked among one another like a mass of human bodies. The church was nearly dark; while the altar, seen far off through a cylinder of darkness, glowed with a soft phosphorescence.

As he wept, Yul felt something like a purring of the floor, while an uncertain but penetrative odor filtered about him. The marble was warm, so that he lay flat on his back and sent his eyes into the shadows of the beams.

The odor increased, until Yul felt a restlessness come over him. He arose, and began putting aside his clothes, until finally he stood naked in the middle of the vast, empty church. Then, listening with great intensity, he thought he could distinguish footsteps. They were far away, but hurrying. They would increase, then nearly fall away completely, so that Yul began to despair. But finally they became firmer; they were advancing; they were upon him . . . and down to one side of the altar he saw a form coming toward him.

While it was still far off, Yul could already distinguish two eyes, which were like moist planets shined on by the sun. That is, they seemed to lie on the face, with an aggressive clearness; while they did not burn but had rather that quiet, steel-blue light of a planet. Of a moist planet, that is . . . not of some dry planets which are like a copper-red spark. Yul watched the eyes, as they came nearer to him, like magnets.

And as the form stood before him, Yul saw that it was the form of a woman; and at once he loved her clamorously. But she picked up the clothes which he had thrown off and held them out to him, so that Yul put them all back upon his body. When he had dressed, he stood in front of her, and looked into her eyes. They were big and deep, like lakes, for he could see down into the rich black pupils as though they really were made of water. She took him by the hand and led him toward the altar, until Yul threw back his head and sang. But his notes began lingering and grumbling to one another among the beams, so that he quit singing. . . . He was led to the edge of the altar. Then she let go his hand, and jumped. Looking where she had jumped, Yul saw that she had leapt across a pit in the center of the altar. He looked down into this pit; it was dark, but so far below that it made him shudder he could see the incandescence of the lowest of the buried cities. Then he jumped and followed his companion on the other side of the altar.

For a time they labored along together, down steps into cold damp places; around sudden bends into rooms which were warm and brilliant; through some narrow passage with a rough, pebbly bottom; then across a little stone bridge under which a spring flowed out of the rock and back into it. But of a sudden she stopped and opened her arms to him. Yul closed against her, looking into the roads and caverns of her eyes. She stepped away, tore back her garments with one fling of her hand . . . and Yul crumpled on the ground under the impact of his disgust. For shining out upon the hairs of the *mons Veneris,* there was a third eye, which beheld him steadily and without blinking.

. . . When Yul awoke, the woman had gone. He began working his way slowly back through the labyrinth of rooms and passages. At last he came upon the pit, and jumped across it. He saw as he went out of the church that immediately in front of it was the broad stairway which led down into the other cities. He looked along the narrowing avenue of stairs, and at the end of them he could make out something which moved. But a peculiar sickness was on him; he longed for his own country, and dropping where he stood, he fell asleep on the first of the granite stairs.

Part Three

Later Yul returned to the stone church . . . and the assembled multitude, lifting its thin voices, chanted in unison the Litany of Error:

> We shall go into the tenth city
>   Glory glory unto our woes
> And take the hands of our fathers
>   Glory glory unto our woes
> And kiss the nail holes in their palms
>   Glory glory unto our woes
> And in the palms of our mothers
>   Glory glory unto our woes
> And touch the old shells of their skin
>   Glory glory unto our woes

And rejoice that now they are alive oh unfolding of the revelation oh ecstasy of blossoming into a world of eternity oh astonishment of opening their petals in the warm garden of our Maker glory glory unto the woes of our fathers and our fathers before them and whatever may befall us in our own day.

The multitude, and the priest . . . they had alternated, the priest alone, standing in the glow of the altar, carrying the "Glory glory unto our woes." But when the lob-end of the prayer was reached, the priest and the kneeling multitude rose up, while heavy music was suddenly sprayed into the church. After the singing was ended, the music wound on for a few bars in reminiscence . . . then it suddenly regained its vigor, and while the multitude knelt again with bowed heads it repeated the entire form of the litany, growing at the last into a tangle of chromatics, with agitated notes crawling in among one another, and accumulating fugues, while the whole jumbled mass grew more voluminous and climbed slowly up the scale. Out of it all there burst one neat, soft chord, high in the treble. This chord hung, while the rest of the music dropped away, until finally it existed all by itself. Then it, too, gradually weakened. But for a long time after it was gone entirely, the multitude remained kneeling.

Now the ceremony seemed to drop more into the business of worship. At times the multitude would rise, kneel at times, while there were even times when it became prostrate on the white marble floor. Up from out of the altar, a long sermon was delivered by one of the priests. It was a well-wrought sermon: it showed the effects of a mind which had devoted long nights to working out the arabesques of its idea. "That which is created creates in turn that by which it was created." The voice from the glowing altar suffered its little elations, its momentary discoveries, its occasional felicities between the idea and the expression thereof . . . the words spread out over the quiet multitude, certain sounds lodging among the beams of the ceiling, others shooting straight to the ear, others floating up sluggishly . . . so that it all became slightly confused and mellow . . . in spite of the hard little stones of the priest's inexorable logic . . . and the voice rose and fell, went slower in places for the purpose of emphasis, hurried across parenthetical explanations, paused before launching on new developments of the idea, halted and retracted a statement to a degree, dropped into a steady trot of exposition . . . the multitude, far from being disturbed that the words of it all did not reach them with clarity, rested comfortably on the dips and fluxes of the priest's voice.

The sermon was followed by a prayer . . . in trailing sentences of unequal length . . . some short . . . some stretching out to the length of two breaths . . . and at the end the multitude joined with the priest in praying . . . the frail single line of words from the altar, then the confused growl of the multitude. After the prayer, the church lay lifeless for a few moments.

Then a flash of light shot across it. The priest climbed in leaps upon the altar, until he stood looking down upon the multitude. A chord was struck, and the priest, taking his pitch immediately as the chord vanished, chanted:

LET THE NINE CHOSEN BE BROUGHT INTO THE HOLY ARENA

And off somewhere, lost in the caverns of the church which led away to the right behind the altar, the chant was repeated in a little thread of voice:

> Let the Nine Chosen be brought into the holy arena.
> Then even fainter, away to the left behind the altar:
> *Holy . . . Holy . . . Holy . . .*
> LET THE NINE CHOSEN BE BOUND UPON THE BEAMS OF THEIR CROSSES
> Let the Nine Chosen be bound upon the beams of their crosses.
> *Crosses . . . crosses . . . crosses of holiness . . .*
> LET THE NAILS BE DRIVEN INTO THE HANDS AND THE FEET OF THEM AND THEIR SIDES TRANSFIXED WITH SPEAR HEADS UNTIL BLOOD MIXES WITH THE SWEAT OF THE EXECUTIONERS AND REJOICE THAT NOW THEY ARE ALIVE OH UNFOLDING OF THE REVELATION OH ECSTASY OF BLOSSOMING INTO A WORLD OF ETERNITY OH ASTONISHMENT OF OPENING THEIR PETALS IN THE WARM GARDEN OF OUR MAKER GLORY GLORY UNTO THE WOES OF OUR FATHERS AND OUR FATHERS BEFORE THEM . . . AND LO! BEHOLD THEM ENTER!

The voice stopped; the priest's arms were stretched out in imitation of the agony of the cross; music broke out, while at the same time a shrieking rose to the right of the altar; silk streamers began dropping and twisting, played upon by lights of all colors. The college of priests hurried up before the altar, howling "Glory, glory!" leaning forward and bearing the crosses of the Nine Crucified like banners. They stopped short before the pit; the music dropped away; the streamers subsided into a lazy billow; the lights became one penetrating reddish purple, which lay in all corners of the church like a sunset. The bodies of the Nine Crucified could be seen moving in silence on their crosses. . . . The priest, from the summit of the altar, gave a signal with his hand, and the crosses with their burdens were dropped into the pit. For a time they could be heard, scraping now and then against the sides, or colliding with one another. Finally, as they reached the bottom of the lowest city, faint thumps came up out of the pit.

The multitude huddled together, closer about the altar. It seemed to be listening. The thumps became heavier; they recurred at set intervals, like a slow treading of feet. Outside the church, beheld by no one in all the city, the march of the armless giants . . . advancing down the broad stairway which was the width of a palace in Yul's own country . . . little ripples passing along their ranks and being lost in the distance . . . armless giants, which rise up boldly out of their legs, like towers.

From *The White Oxen And Other Stories* (New York: Albert & Charles Boni, 1924), pp. 193-211.

Lexicon Rhetoricae

(*1931*)

Ritual

25. *Ideology*. Expanding our earlier discussion of ideology: If people believe something, the poet can use this belief to get an effect. If they despise treachery, for instance, he can awaken their detestation by the portrait of a traitor. If they admire self-sacrifice, he can set them to admiring by a tragedy of self-sacrifice. If they hold the earth the center of the universe, he can base the dignity of man upon geocentricity. By an ideology is meant the nodus of beliefs and judgments which the artist can exploit for his effects. It varies from one person to another, and from one age to another—but insofar as its general acceptance and its stability are more stressed than its particular variations from person to person and from age to age, an ideology is a "culture." If an entire nation feels abhorrence at the profaning of a certain kind of altar, and agrees as to how the altar could be profaned, to that extent it possesses a "culture." But there are cultures within cultures, since a society can be subdivided into groups with divergent standards and interests. Each of these subdivisions of a culture may possess its own characteristic ideology (contrast the ideology of a young radical in the coal mines with the ideology of a retired banker touring the Mediterranean), but in so far as they overlap they belong to the same culture (both the radical and the banker, for instance, may despise an informer). Generally, the ideology of an individual is a slight variant of the ideology distinguishing the class among which he arose.

The artist obtains his effects by manipulating our ideological assumptions in many ways. The simplest is "idealization," as when a Symbol so thoroughly exemplifies the pitiable that we can be thoroughly aroused to pity. In general, his effects are obtained by the playing of some assumptions against others (the author of "The King and the Peasant," who would show that real kingliness can be found in peasants, and kings can be boors, does this by pitting the assumptions of spiritual distinction against the assumptions of social distinction). Tragedy is based upon the firm acceptance of an ideology (an author can most ably arouse our grief over the death of a hero when he and we are in complete agreement as to what qualities are heroic). For this reason perhaps the humorous writers are better equipped today than the tragic ones, since humor results from a discrepancy between ideological assumptions, and the great conflict of standards in contemporary society gives the artist a considerable range of such discrepancies to select from. Thus when Will Rogers, in commenting on the presence of U.S. Marines in Nicaragua, said: "All this trouble about Nicaragua—why don't they come out and fight us like a man?" he was, in so dealing with the discrepancy between the power of the United States and the power of the "enemy," attaining humor by pitting the assumptions of sportsmanship (we should choose an opponent our size) against the assumptions of patriotism (our country always in the right).

Many of the beliefs exploited by poetry in the past were backed by the authority of the Church; in the future, beliefs may be to a great extent founded upon science. There is perhaps no essential difference between religious and scientific "foundations," however, as religion is probably the outgrowth of magic, itself a "science" based on theories of causation which were subsequently modified or discredited. Magic, religion, and science are alike in that they foster a body of thought concerning the nature of the universe and man's relation to it. All three offer possibilities to the artist in so far as they tend to make some beliefs prevalent or stable.

An ideology is not a harmonious structure of beliefs or assumptions; some of its beliefs militate against others, and some of its standards militate against our nature. An ideology is an aggregate of beliefs sufficiently at odds with one another to justify opposite kinds of conduct. Thus, the artist's patterns of experience may be manifest in his particular stressing of the ideology. Accepting certain assumptions or beliefs as valid, he will exploit them to discredit other assumptions or beliefs which he considers invalid. He may, for instance, exploit assumptions of individual dignity to attack the assumptions that we must without protest obey the king. He may use the assumptions of natural beauty to rout the industrialist's assumptions of progress—or vice versa. It is by such aligning of assumptions that poetry contributes to the formation of attitudes, and thus to the determining of conduct.

26. *The Symbolically and formally "charged."* Intensity in art may be attributed sometimes to form, sometimes to the Symbol, sometimes to both. Symbolic intensity arises when the artist uses subject matter "charged" by the reader's situation outside the work of art. Thus: the portrait of a spy in war times—the account of a seduction, in books for adolescents. (It is told that when Spain was lethargically enduring an unpopular dictatorship, and had suffered for several years without rebellion, a vaudeville actor in a Madrid theatre opened his act by having the curtain rise on an empty stage. The stage remained empty for some time, while the audience grew more and more impatient. Finally, when they were protesting furiously, the actor appeared. He held up his hand for silence; the audience subsided; and he spoke rebukingly: "I don't see why you couldn't wait a few minutes. You have been waiting now for seven years." This remark was Symbolically "charged." Its ominous humor depended upon a current political situation in Spain. Alter the situation of the audience, and the witticism falls flat, becoming almost meaningless.) Often, to "charge" his work Symbolically, a writer strains to imagine some excessive horror, not because he is especially addicted to such imaginings, but because the prevalence of similar but less extreme Symbols has impaired their effectiveness. He may plumb the depths of sadism or incest when seeking no more than what an earlier writer sought in the tale of a naive courtship. If he would avoid the procedure, he must Symbolize new patterns,

or use new modes of experience in the Symbolizing of old patterns, or attempt to increase accuracy and range. To an extent, all subject matter is categorically "charged," in that each word relies for its meaning upon a social context, and thus possesses values independently of the work in which it appears. Symbolic charge, therefore, is but a matter of degree.

Formal charges may be attributed to arrangements within the work itself. Though a writer were to feel dismal but seldom, if he had stored the many aspects of his dismalness and put them into a single work, such use of repetitive form could give the impression of a world corroded by dismalness from morning till night. Or if a writer so arranges his plot that the words "I am here" have a pronounced bearing upon the course of his story, the utterance of these simple words may have a tremendous influence upon the audience. Consider, in Racine's *Iphigénie*, the speech of Arcas, when he enters to announce that the time for Iphigenia's sacrifice is at hand. Up to this point, Iphigenia has been making arrangements for her marriage; she, her mother, her suitor, and her rival now learn for the first time that she is not to be married, but to be slain. The function of syllogistic progression in "charging" the words of Arcas is obvious.

As for the clear collaboration of both formal and Symbolic charge:

The description of a terrific storm is Symbolically charged. It relies for its effect upon our attitudes towards storms independently of the particular work in which this description appears. But, through the workings of qualitative progression, the description of a terrific storm may become more imposing if it follows, say, the account of a very effete scene in a salon. Or an image suggesting the vastness of a mountain may be reinforced by a peculiarity of rhythm, by a stressing of assonance, or by some saliency in the word order. (The two kinds of charge, of course, are never wholly separable.)

27. *Eloquence*. Eloquence is a frequency of Symbolic and formal effects. One work is more eloquent than another if it

contains Symbolic and formal charges in greater profusion. That work would be most eloquent in which each line had some image or statement relying strongly upon our experience outside the work of art, and in which each image or statement had a pronounced formal saliency.

We might contrast Stendhal and Shakespeare. The Symbol underlying *Le Rouge et le Noir* owes much of its effectiveness to its summarizing of certain volitionalist doctrines which were incipient in Stendhal's day but have since come to fruition. Also, the work in which this Symbol appears is marked by an exceptionally capable handling of repetitive form and syllogistic progression. The individual lines, however, are by definite program "non-eloquent." For their effect they depend entirely upon their place in the whole. A conversation in Stendhal is not interesting as conversation; it is interesting exactly as a conversation might be interesting in real life: because of its bearing upon the future. It is interesting as an actual quarrel between two lovers might be interesting to themselves—not because a single phrase of any brilliance was spoken, but because each sentence was important to the lovers' relationship. Each sentence in Stendhal deliberately eschews any saliency as a minor or incidental form—it aims to be imperceptible—and if the reader forgets that he is reading, he is reading as Stendhal would have him read.

The "eloquent" principle, as exemplified by Shakespeare, is a constant attempt to renew Symbolic and formal appeal throughout the work. Each ramification of the Symbol must depend for its effectiveness not merely upon its functions as a subdivision of the Symbol (repetitive form)—it must be an image or statement containing Symbolic appeal in itself. It must, that is, bring up some picture, or summarize some situation, or in some other way recommend itself as an independent value. Or it must contain some oddity of sound or rhythm which gives it an independent claim to our attention. Thus, by the principle of "eloquence," a conversation would not merely reiterate the identity of the speakers and contribute to the course of the plot—it would also be interesting as conversation.

28. *Manner and Style.* Insofar as a work becomes eloquent, it manifests either manner or style. Here again the distinction is quantitative, manner being a greater confinement of formal resources and Symbolic ramifications. Oscar Wilde's *Salome* is an example of manner. (The ramifications of the Symbol have a very limited range, bearing almost wholly upon the stressing of decadent desire. Formally, the work is a constant repetition of the *non sequitur:* the significance of the characters' statements is brought out formally by the perverse refusal of these characters to answer one another—they converse, but in monologue, and the most important questions are followed by an abrupt changing of the subject as the person replying pursues his own line of thought.) As an instance of style, we might consider the later prose of Shakespeare, with its range of imagery and formulation, and its abundance of diverse incidental forms. (This style approaches manner in so far as it overemphasizes metaphor.)

Manner obviously has the virtue of "power," with the danger of monotony (*Salome* may illustrate both). Style has the virtue of "complexity," with the danger of diffusion. (The later prose of James Joyce is a good instance of style impaired by diffusion.)

29. *The "categorical appeal" of literature.* Eloquence, by stressing the means of literature, requires an interest in the means as ends. Otherwise eloquence becomes an obstacle to enjoyment. Readers who seek in art a substitute for living will find the Stendhal procedure most acceptable; a novelist like the Hugo of *L'Homme Qui Rit* will annoy them with his bristling epigrammatic "unreality," a kind of saliency so thoroughly literary that, however strong the readers' impressions, they can never forget that the book is "written." Nor would Hugo want us to forget that his book was "written." The primary purpose of eloquence is not to enable us to live our lives on paper—it is to convert life into its most thorough verbal equivalent. The categorical appeal of literature resides in a liking for verbalization as such, just as the categorical appeal

of music resides in a liking for musical sounds as such. The stressing of a medium requires a preference for this medium— and thus in eloquence, which is the maximum stressing of the literary medium, we may find evidence of a "categorical appeal."

30. *"Esthetic" truth.* The relation between "scientific" and "esthetic" truth might be likened to the relation between revelation and ritual. Revelation is "scientific," whether its "truth" be founded upon magic, religion, or laboratory experiment. Revelation is "belief," or "fact." Art enters when this revelation is ritualized, when it is converted into a symbolic process. We treat with ceremony a fact considered of importance (if we consider a thing distinguished, we surround it with other things which we consider distinguished: we touch a "pure" object with "clean" hands). Art as eloquence, ceremony, ritual, is nothing other than this principle of consistency, of matching the important with the important. If the artist's "revelations" are of tremendous importance to him, he will necessarily seek to ritualize them, to find a correspondingly important setting for them.

But the ritualizing of a revelation does not merely produce revelation plus ritual. A kind of metaphorical truth enters. The artist, for instance, when he has converted his pattern of experience into a corresponding Symbol, finds himself with many problems which do not concern this pattern of experience at all. He will then treat this Symbol in ways which, from the standpoint of the underlying pattern, are "untrue." He may, for instance, though deeply opposed to religious dogma, write sympathetically of an imaginary religious service based wholly upon the most extreme kinds of dogma. Here truth is not "scientific," but "metaphorical." The "thoughts" of a writer are not the mere "revelation," not the statement of a fact—the "thoughts" are the framing of this revelation in ritual. Accordingly, our savants err who attempt to catalogue for us the "thoughts" of a stylist like Milton, by stating them simply as precepts divorced from their stylistic context. The "thoughts" of a writer are the non-paraphrasable aspects of his work, the revelation and the ritual in fusion. So greatly does the ritual-istic element figure in the artist's mechanism, that he might rather ritualize a pattern of experience not wholly expressive of him than symbolize a pattern which he could not convert into ritual (as Mark Twain, who would preferably have been tragic, confined his formal writings to humor). It is this primary concern with "esthetic" truth which has exposed the poet, even in his own eyes, to the charge of insincerity, and thus led him to attempt glorifying the charge. (The "insincerity" of putting one's children in an orphan asylum and writing a work on education—the "insincerity" of going to southern France and singing of Wisconsin—the "insincerity" of getting an effect by the use of an assumption which the artist himself often doubts.) A poet may base an effect upon a belief which he knows to be false, just as he may compose a poem on riding to the moon; in either case he writes "as if" the underlying fact were true.

Ritual, ceremony, eloquence, esthetic truth, the non-para-phrasable, the metaphorical, the factually "insincere." (Ritual is to revelation as Lucretius is to Democritus. The "esthetic truth" of Dr. Johnson's assertiveness becomes more apparent as the "scientific truth" of his assertions diminishes—Boswell's Johnson becomes a character out of Dickens.)

31. *Eloquence and the traditionally ceremonious.* The great danger in eloquence resides in the fact that it tends to become not a quantitative but a qualitative thing. The ritualizing of a revelation, that is, tends to confine itself to certain usages traditionally ceremonious. For if the artist would place his important revelation in an important setting, what more natural than that he should select for his setting such ideas as are tradi-tionally considered important? Eloquence thus comes to be allied with strict doctrines of inclusion and exclusion. It utilizes the traditionally dignified, overlooking the fact that any tradi-tionally dignified word or image or "thought" is dignified not through an intrinsic quality but because earlier artists made it so. By laying emphasis upon the categorical appeal of art,

eloquence threatens to make poetry "derivative," to make it develop out of itself rather than out of the situations of life. The poet thus derives his Symbolic charges from the Symbolic charges of his poetic forbears. In writing a "wouldst-thou" love poem today, the poet would be obtaining eloquence by the weakened method we have in mind, though the mistake is not always so obvious.

Eloquence, by our definition, would not be situated in such rigid distinctions between "good taste" and "bad taste." It would, rather, be a matter of profusion. The artist shows his respect for his subject, not by laying a wreath at its feet, but by the fullness of his preoccupation with it. The soundness of his concerns will be manifested either in exceptional variety or in exceptional accurateness. Now, if this profusion could be got from past literature alone, there could be no objection to so getting it. But it happens to require such intensity and spontaneity of purpose as can arise only out of situations in life itself. Thus, the artist whose eloquence is an eloquence of profusion, will base his inclusions and exclusions not on traditional definitions of the ceremonious, but upon those aspects of an ideology which can be associated with the ceremonious in his environment. His eloquence will be based upon the contemporaneously charged, rather than upon the traditionally charged. To an extent, of course, the contemporary charge will be a survival of the traditional—but there are new elements (in both ideology and "living") to which the traditional is not accurately adapted.

Universality, Permanence, Perfection

32. *Recurrent patterns of experience.* There are some stock patterns of experience which seem to arise out of any system of living. Thus: the dramatic irony of digging one's own grave (Bellerophontic letter); the return of youth (Faust legend, "the man who came back"); persecution at the hands of those whom one would benefit (Christ legend); slight cause leading

to disproportionately grave effect ("The Piece of String");
Judas psychology (poignancy of harming a friend—Agamemnon
sacrificing his daughter—Brutus conspiring against Caesar for
the good of the state); Utopia; *per aspera ad astra* (attainment after difficulty). One will find the Symbols for such patterns recurring throughout all literature. However, the Symbols, with their ramifications, vary greatly—and may not be
effective though the underlying pattern applies strongly to the
reader. Consider the many avid readers of the *per aspera ad
astra* pattern as symbolized in our modern "success literature."
Despite their eagerness, they would find little to entice them in
this same pattern as symbolized by the *Quest of the Golden
Fleece*. Pain at loss is universal—yet A will be greatly pained
at the loss of something which B never had and never felt the
need of having. Similarly, *Marius the Epicurean* and *The
Doll's House* are concerned with fundamentally the same pattern—transition, the transvaluation of values. Ibsen symbolizes
the pattern by modes of experience specifically applicable to
the households of his audience. Pater symbolizes the pattern by
modes of experience applicable to a post-Darwinian scholar of
Greco-Roman classics. Though symbolizing a pattern of experience common to many, he symbolizes it by modes of experience exceptional to most. In both cases we have a pattern
to which people in modern times are sensitive; yet the symbol-
izations of this pattern are so different that a certain kind of
reader could praise Ibsen for "dealing with life" and condemn
Pater for "unreality." As the situation changes, the Pater Symbol may as likely as not be found the more apposite of the two,
since it does not rely upon so specific a "charge" as the early
feminist movement gave to Ibsen's Symbol.

Thus, though a pattern of experience could be proved universal (common to all men) or permanent (common to some
men in every age), the work of art in which it is symbolized
would not be thereby proved universal or permanent.

33. *Fluctuant factors affecting the Symbol.* The appeal of
the Symbol may be impaired by the following factors:

Variations in ideology. (An author, to make us admire a character, may endow the character with traits admirable by the author's code but not admirable by the reader's code. What Dickens considered the height of female virtue the reader may consider exceptional unimaginativeness. If picturing a sorry specimen of boyhood for Spartans, don't picture him as a thief.)

Remoteness of patterns (Baudelaire's preoccupations with purification through sin will have little to do with the preoccupations of a sales promoter at peace with his calling).

Divergence of modes (as illustrated by the Ibsen-Pater distinction, the different significance of snow to a Greenlander and snow to a Roman). Obviously, the line of demarcation between modes and patterns of experience is vague. A pattern is perhaps definable as a particular stressing of a mode. The details of life in the city would be *modes* of experience—a constant irritation at life in the city would be a *pattern* of experience. The modes would be the particular details with which this irritation was associated—as the irritation of a subway jam, of dodging automobiles, of early morning noises.

Degree of familiarity. (A Symbol may become ineffective, not through any fundamental lack of appositeness, but simply because too many others have used the same Symbol. To sing hey-nonny-nonny effectively, one would now have to sing something else.) Also, the degree of familiarity with a pattern affects our judgment of the Symbol for this pattern. A person to whom the pattern is remote may need more obvious ramifications to be affected, whereas a person to whom the pattern is close might find many such obvious ramifications too blunt. (Contrast talk between two experts with talk between an expert and a layman. In talking with a layman, the expert will necessarily stress some of the very points which he would be most likely to omit in talking with another expert.)

34. *Formal obstacles.* We have previously indicated how progressive and repetitive form are affected by the casualties of subject matter. Our analysis of eloquence (style and man-

ner) now equips us to consider the possible alienation of readers through conventional form, or "categorical expectancy." Elizabethan audiences, through expecting the bluster of the proscenium speech, found it readily acceptable—but a modern audience not schooled in this expectation will object to it as "unreal." Yet this same audience will find nothing to resent in a kind of banter or smart repartee which is, so far as life itself is concerned, equally "unreal." The obstacle in conventional form arises from the fact that conventions militate against one another. The conventions of post-Ibsen drama, for instance, *do not merely omit* the Greek chorus; they *"demand" the omission* of the Greek chorus, one of the most effective mechanisms in the history of drama thereby being categorically eschewed.

The distinction between style and manner is also fluctuant, as a change in conventional form can make one aspect of a style very noticeable and thus give it the effect of manner. In the age of Pope, the metaphor of Shakespeare was disliked because of its conceptual weakness: in the interests of picturesqueness, it permitted itself to become intellectually inaccurate. The Imagists, on the other hand, disliked the Shakespearean metaphor because it was *too conceptual, too intellectual!* They preferred the suppression of the logical connectives which this metaphor always revealed. Thus to two other schools the Shakespearean metaphor, which was "natural" enough in its day, became an obstructive mannerism.

A maladjustment of conventional form can also arise from the pattern of experience. The reader who is, let us say, of a flighty, bustling nature, may require writing of the same sort. The diction "natural" to him will be composed of short, behavioristic sentences, with few modifiers. The leisurely, meditative manner of a Proust, or the complex solemnity of a De Quincey, will necessarily alienate him. He approaches art with a categorical demand for a specific kind of eloquence; which is to say, a pronounced pattern of experience will lead him to demand one specific manner of writing, and will by the same token make other manners or styles unsuitable to his enjoyment. Flaubert was pleased to think that he had accom-

modated his sentences to the human respiration, so that pauses
fell at breathing spaces, though he did not specify whether he
had in mind the short-breathed and apoplectic or the even
respiratory performances of a trained singer. Most persons
would be insensitive to any influence by such means, since
they read with a minimum of auditory imaginings; but as for
persons who may be sensitive to literary values of this kind,
if Flaubert's respiratory pauses can give pleasure to a reader
whose speed of breathing and reading corresponds with the
speed to which the author's page is accommodated, for the
same reason they might give displeasure to a reader in whom
this correspondence was lacking.

35. *Compensatory gains.* A work, in ceasing to be apposite for the reasons previously described, need not thereby
cease to appeal. There are extrinsic aspects of appeal. Thus,
through the passing of Latin, Virgil takes on a sepulchral
dignity not there for his contemporaries. Among such compensatory gains are: antiquity (the appeal of a work removed
in time); quaintness (the appeal of a work removed in custom, or ideology); absurdity (the appeal of a work through
its sheer error, the work being "efficient enough in its bad-
ness" to make a virtue of its defects); typicality (the appeal
of a work because it is representative, or symptomatic, of
certain critical theories, as the appeal of a work "because it
is representative of nineteenth-century England"); rarity (the
appeal of a work because there are few works of its kind);
picturesqueness (appeal of an attitude which, being alien to
the reader, furnishes him with a "fresh" way of seeing things.
Thus, though the author be very guileless, if he happens to
write out of a social or emotional situation greatly different
from the reader's, his work may become the equivalent of
great inventiveness or ingenuity. It is in this way that primitive
works often appeal to us, delighting us as a vehicle for "artistic"
effects, giving us the sense of the dextrous that we get in the
depiction of Falstaff). In general, the work possesses extrinsic
appeal when its appeal resides in the reader's failure to

duplicate the experience intended by the author. (A "realistic" account of life in Tibet will appeal as a "romantic" book to Occidentals; what one man loves as doxology another may admire for its uniqueness.)

Again, works invalidated as "scientific" truth may take on appeal as "esthetic" truth. The disproving of Democritus does not invalidate the doctrines of Democritus as "poetized" in Lucretius' *De Rerum Natura*. Plato and Spinoza, whose doctrines, in their literal meaning, are endangered, survive as "artists," their questioned "scientific" truth being embalmed as "esthetic" truth. The blunt certainties of a Dr. Johnson gain as "esthetic" truth, the more thoroughly they are undermined as "scientific" truth. One may enjoy these certainties as a "tonic" for his many modern doubts. Thus, though Johnson, as the Symbol of Boswell's *Life*, ceases to appeal as the summarizing of a situation, he appeals as the adjustment to a situation.

Similarly, conventional form can appeal through its sheer divorce from contemporary expectations. The very reader who would object if someone wrote today in the eighteenth-century manner may find this manner of great appeal in an eighteenth-century writer.

36. *Margin of persuasion.* "Compensatory gains" occur when the Symbol appeals for reasons extrinsic to the author's intentions. By the "margin of persuasion" we refer to the means whereby the author can reduce the recalcitrant reader to acquiescence, the means whereby the Symbol, though remote from the reader, can be made to appeal for reasons intrinsic to the author's intention.

First, there is the authority of the expert. The artist possessed by a certain pattern of experience is an "expert" in this pattern. He should thus be equipped to make it convincing, for the duration of the fiction at least. By thoroughness he should be able to overwhelm his reader and thus compel the reader to accept his interpretations. For a pattern of experience is an interpretation of life. Life being open to many interpretations, the reader is open to many interpretations. Only the madman or the genius or the temporarily exalted (as the lover, the terrified, or the sick) will have a pattern of experience so pronounced as to close him to the authority of other patterns of experience. The thoroughness of the artist's attack can "wear down" the reader until he accepts the artist's interpretation, the pattern of experience underlying the Symbol. He may, when the book is finished, return to his own contrary patterns of experience forthwith (but during the reading the evidence has been rigorously selected, it "points" as steadily in one direction as the contentions of a debater).

This "margin of persuasion" is further made possible by the fact that our modes of experience are ambiguous or fluctuant. That is, the normal person has a variety of feelings attached to the same object. A thundershower can cause terror if one is caught far from shore in a rowboat, or relief if it tempers the heat. A locomotive can cause terror if on-rushing, or relief if it takes us away from an unsatisfactory environment. Thus the artist, who attempts to convey emotions by drawing upon the modes of experience connected with such emotions, could use locomotives and storms to convey emotions as unlike as terror and relief. Have the train onrushing, with a car stalled on the tracks in a violent downpour, and "storm-locomotive" conveys terror; have the hero break clear of his troubles by flight, have him settle back comfortably in a Pullman chair as the train moves quietly out of the station, with the storm, after the oppressive sultriness of the day, causing a cool wind to blow down the aisle, and "storm-locomotive" conveys relief. Thus, the fluctuant quality in our modes of experience provides a neutral or ambiguous territory which the artist can "weight," which he can by his selective methods endow with a pattern.

This neutral or ambiguous territory serves the artist in another way. Many of his sharpest perceptions, his most convincing images, or the most skillful trends in the treatment of his plots, are not exclusively allied with his particular pattern of experience. The same inventions could have arisen out of some other pattern of experience. Thus, the author can inveigle his reader by the rich use of this "neutral" territory. Byron may appeal to the Byronic by his Byronism— but to a certain non-Byronic reader he may have to appeal, say, by such qualities of natural observation as ally him with Shelley.

We must also consider the value of formal appeal in inducing acquiescence. For to guide the reader's expectations is already to have some conquest over him. Thus even a rhythm not categorically adapted to the reader (he may prefer swifter ones or slower ones or more voluminous ones, etc.) can increase its adaptability through the patient pervasiveness of repetitive form.

The "margin of persuasion" is the region of corrosion, corrosion obtained by thoroughness, thoroughness manifest either as accuracy, or as profusion, or as both.

37. *Perfection.* Enough has been said to demonstrate that "perfection" as applied to literature is a meaningless term. The naturalness of progressive and repetitive form is impaired by divergence in the ideologies of writer and reader (the writer cannot arouse us to vindictiveness by an act which, though he considers it despicable, we happen to consider pitiable, as certain kinds of "wickedness" are now condoned as "insanity"). The work can very easily be maladjusted from the standpoint of conventional form, if it fails to coincide with our expectations (a work may have much stylistic vigor, but the very eloquence of the diction will militate against it if the reader "categorically" requires simple narrative statement). The hypertrophy or atrophy of any principle can be effective or obstructive, depending upon the bias of the reader. The same Symbol appeals to different readers for different reasons: (1) because there is a similarity of writer's and reader's pattern (a Byronic Symbol appealing to a "mute Byron"); or (2) because the writer by his thoroughness compels the reader to accept his interpretation (a Poe horror story making a joyous man feel uneasy); or (3) by "compensatory gains" (as

the free thinker De Gourmont delighted in the early poetry of the Church). Again, the pattern underlying the Symbol can be obscured by the modes of experience employed in the ramifying of the Symbol (songs about the merry month of May would hardly fit as a greeting to spring in Tierra del Fuego; one cannot awaken a sense of strangeness in the reader by talking of Xanadu, if the reader happens to be Kubla Khan).

Perfection could exist only if the entire range of the reader's and the writer's experience were identical down to the last detail. Universal and permanent perfection could exist only if this entire range of experiences were identical for all men forever.

To have "perfection," we should need a "perfect reader" to whom such perfection could be referred. That is, we should have to specify some definite pattern of experience as the "ideal" pattern of experience. Should a warlike work of art, for instance, be so written as to stir the patriotic, or so written as to stir the antipatriotic (in the first case we might arouse the audience by depicting the brutalities of the national enemy, in the second we might arouse the audience by depicting the machinations of our own munitions makers). Should the work of art appeal to the humiliated, the indignant, the suffering—or should it appeal to those who, either by good fortune or by some deep "philosophy," have acquired repose? Obviously, the work of art can appeal to either—and in appealing most fully to one, it prejudices its appeal to the other. Reducing the problem to its simplest terms, Aristotle points out in his *Rhetoric* that there are friendly audiences, hostile audiences, and simply curious audiences, the orator's problems differing in accordance with the type of audience he is addressing. Such divisions apply as rigorously to the Symbols of poetry and fiction as to any subjects of abstract debate. To speak of a work as "perfect," we should have to establish one of these audiences as the point of reference.

As a kind of hypothetical norm, we might divide our readers

into the "hysteric" and the "connoisseur." The hysteric will demand in art a Symbol which is "medicinal" to his situation. He will require one very specific kind of art. Insofar as the reader approaches the hypothetical state of the connoisseur, he is open to the appeal of all Symbols, but is overwhelmed by none. He will approach art *as art,* thus requiring the maximum of ritualization, verbalization. He will be "will-less," "hunger-less," going to art for nothing but art itself. He will require not one specific kind of art (as the hysteric, who must have only detective stories, or murder stories, or success fiction) but any art profuse in technical happenings. The actual reader is obviously an indeterminate and fluctuant mixture of these two extremes. An art might be said to approach "perfection" in proportion as its appeal is made to the second kind of reader—but in all purity he could not possibly exist. Every word a writer uses depends for its very "meaning" upon the reader's previous experience with the object or situation which the word suggests. That is to say, the word is "charged" by the reader's own experiences, and to this extent the reader is "hysteric." "Madness" is but meaning carried to the extreme.

Or we might limit the matter, calling a work perfect if it attains its ends—a patriotic work being in a broad sense perfect if it is written for patriots and moves patriots, and an anti-patriotic play being perfect if it is written for antipatriots and moves antipatriots. (For those who would say that the antipatriotic play can also move patriots, I should but ask them to consider producing such a play in war times. It can move patriots in times of peace, *when their patriotism has weakened:* in other words, it can move them insofar as they are *not* patriots.) Thus, we can only preserve "perfection" in this sense: "a perfect work for girls of seventeen who are living in small provincial towns in 1931, are not very well educated, are dissatisfied with their surroundings, and dream of a career in Hollywood," or "a perfect work for people with six toes, this spring." We can save the concept of perfection only by making it of no critical value. If a work of art were perfectly adapted to one situation, by this very fact its chances of subsequent perfection would be eliminated, as the identical situation will not recur.

*   *   *

39. *Uplift. How eloquence leads to uplift:* The profuse embodiment of eloquence cannot be accomplished without coexisting discipline (resistance) and exposure (nonresistance). The poet must manage exposure without collapse, discipline without exclusion. The artist does, of course, tend to develop a "protective" attitude, and he may be content to symbolize it. But in attempting to increase the range of his arguments (the thoroughness of his ramifications), he is pledged to the deepening and widening of his patterns and to the strengthening of his formal contrivances. The expansion of the Symbol, since it is done for the purpose of appeal, involves processes of intellection, or logic (hence the difference between the *passivity* of a dream and the *enterprise* of art).

Value of the aggregate: The great mass of art can produce an effect beyond the range of the individual artists. Were each artist to give us but a restricted pattern, we could get something beyond these experiences out of their assemblage, owing to the conflicts and mutual exclusions. For the sincere artist, the pattern is, within the terms of the fiction at least, as he writes it. For the reader the artist's world may become, at the termination of the fiction, a mere addition to his working hypotheses. The "sum total of art" relieves the artist of the need of seeing life steadily and seeing it whole. He will presumably desire to be as comprehensive as he can, but what he lacks in adjustability can be supplied by another artist affirming some other pattern with equal conviction.

Technical: The exercise of human subtleties and potentialities in a sphere which can be largely noncompetitive. Increase of perception and sensitivity through increase of terminology (a character or a situation in fiction is as much a term as any definition in a scientific nomenclature). An equipment, like any vocabulary, for handling the complexities of living.

Holier than thou: The artist, as artist, will be more concerned with moral imaginings than with moral stability. He must, of course, be able to perceive his refinements for the duration of the saying—but character, in the social sense, is based upon an integrity, or constancy, which an artist—as artist—need not have. If art were a matter of character, rather than of artistic aptitude, it follows that a great painter would also be a great musician, a great novelist, a great architect, etc. Perhaps no man can, by taking thought, add a cubit to his stature; but he clearly can, by revision, remove much that lowers his general average. So we may consider art as bigger than the artist, who can accordingly apply himself to his trade in its noblest aspects with such modesty as befits any standard of human decency. For if the calling is greater than the man, he need not, in the selection of so high a calling, feel himself in the coxcomb's position of standing forth as a moral muster for all mankind.

From *Counter-Statement* (2nd ed.; Los Altos, Calif.: Hermes Publications, 1953), pp. 161-183.

A Story by John Neal

(1932)

My dear,

All day I have been walking the streets in mild despair. In the late afternoon I sat on a bench in one of the small parks, and watched the sun sink. He too, in this mid-September weather, is mild and a little weary. His long debauch of summer has weakened him but I, except for a few miraculous hours not many months past, have known no strong passions to be weak from. Oh, half of my soul, *animae dimidium meae* as our bleary-eyed old Horace put it, let your affection for me do what my affection for myself could never do: let it lead you to forgive this indiscreet wailing. Without you to hear me, I have no one. Of all these millions of people, the single one who has shown me a spark of recognition is a wooden policeman in front of a cigar store nearby, a dummy if there ever was one. He and I are akin, for his waxen dignity, his benign officialdom, is as eternal, as hopelessly inalterable, as my mild despair.

But you see what unhealthy preoccupations I have fallen into. Lampposts, streetcars, gutters have characters for me, when people do not. And as a consequence, I cannot continue my work. I am subdued, and a little dazed. My uprooting has not given me the assistance we thought it would. So you must not delay much longer. For if an occasional quick breath of hope raises this burden of dismalness that is upon me, it is because I dare expect you. Yet I can promise you nothing but the abject tributes of one who loves you "like the little bird that picks up crumbs around the door," if I may quote again a passage from Blake which you have heard me quote so often. I have stood before the glass and told myself: "What claims do you have upon her? By what right could you ask her to come here?" If one must expect much to get a little, how can I encourage you to join me? For if attainments fall short of ambitions, and I dare look forward to nothing, what a ghastly result we have after the substraction!

Yesterday, in spite of my loathing, I forced myself to work at the twelfth chapter, where my hero clearly sees the implications of his character converging upon him. The sort of life he has constructed is becoming inexorably apparent to him. He is lonely, my dear, even as lonely as I—and his loneliness will undo him. He has made himself a Mole, to learn what Eagles cannot imagine. A writer can, out of the depths of himself, invent but one new aspect of vice; no wonder that he prizes it greatly and dignifies it by having it cause the destruction of his hero. So in my behalf, the poor devil must suffer. We have allowed him to retain a kind of sullen optimism, an ill-natured praise of God, but I would not put any faith in the chances of either himself or his author.

Oct. 12

My dear,

If you have not received any letters from me for a couple of weeks, it is not because I have not written to you. No day has passed in which I have not devoted many hours to you. But I have always become ashamed of my complainings, and have destroyed them. Will she ever have us, I have warned myself, if we go on discouraging her with our self-doubts? I thank you that you have not scolded me for my silence. I worked doggedly all day today, despite the repugnance of the task, and succeeded in piling up eight thousand more sluggish words. (Eight thousand more, by count. Remember our Blake: "Bring out number weight & measure in a year of dearth." He knew this curse, through knowing so well the corresponding privilege:

"Every time less than a pulsation of the artery
Is equal in its period & value to Six Thousand Years

For in this Period the Poet's Work is Done, and all the Great
Events of Time start forth & are conceiv'd in such a Period:
Within a Moment, a Pulsation of the Artery."

I read him often now, our Blake. I marvel that he could invent
such "Giant forms" as never were, yet could know beyond
hesitancy how each one looked and how each one would have
spoken. It is only in my letters to you that I am fluent—but
these, in sheer self-protection, I must repeatedly destroy. My
genius resides in loving you abjectly.)

Still, there are compensations. For I was exhausted, and I
swear that I should never touch this desolate work again were
it not that I must earn you, that I must make some visible thing
which entitles me to you. I was exhausted, until my very
tissues drooped with nausea. I fled from my room into the
crisp fall air, hoping only for a physical recovery. But the wind
attacked me, and I walked furiously, tingling. And of a sudden
I understood that something more than mere bodily exaltation
was upon me. "What does the damned book matter," I cried,
"when she will soon be here to comfort me!" I felt again the
prodigal ambitions of those days when you talked with me
and pictured for me the future of both of us. You, I understood,
would make my work prosper. And I felt so very good that
on the way back to my room I could not resist one happy wink
at my friend, the dummy policeman. Indeed, I did more than
that. I noticed that on his pedestal he bore a message recommending a certain brand of cigar. I immediately entered his
store and bought one. It was a wretched cigar, and as you
know I don't care much for even good cigars, but I played
fair, and smoked that cigar to the dregs.

"Dear Mother, dear Mother, the Church is cold,
   But the Ale-house is healthy & pleasant & warm,"

I sang to myself, the little vagabond did sing—for at the
thought of you he had left the gloomy Church of his recalcitrant novel, to sit in the cozy Alehouse of his love. I did not
mind my previous miserableness, since its cure was so
thorough. And I was shamelessly indebted to you. If one has

great distinctness, he will search long before he finds in
another that sweet combination of traits which forms his
precise complement—and if he finds her, is it not reasonable
that he should think of her unceasingly? Oh, do not mistake
me. In speaking of my distinctness, I do not hint at exceptional
abilities. A man would be distinct with noses for ears. I mean
simply that for each lack in me, you brought the corresponding
fulness; that wherever I was in need, you had the fitting kind
of charity. Thirst is a delight where there is water; where
food is plentiful, hunger is a luxury. I did not now regret my
particular ills, since they turned me with such avidity to you
as the cure for them. You recall, in *Jerusalem,* the passage on
Mary's love which we enjoyed so greatly, and how you would
laugh when I insisted that with us the sexes should be
reversed—me Mary, and you Joseph:

> "Then Mary burst forth into a Song: she flowed like a River of
> Many Streams in the arms of Joseph & gave forth her tears of joy
> Like many waters, and Emanating into gardens and palaces
> upon
> Euphrates, & to forests & floods & animals wild & tame from
> Gihon to Hiddekel, & to corn fields & villages & inhabitants
> Upon Pison & Arnon & Jordan . . ."

I felt this expansiveness of Mary. I felt as though I were
pouring forth bounty—is that not funny, when I was silent
even, had not even one sentence to offer, could show nothing
more ambitious than my gratitude to you?

Nov. 7

My dear,
     It would be a relief for me to think that for once I can write
you about something other than myself; and I should be
thankful for this respite were it not caused by the pressure of
a topic equally repellent. How, *animae dimidium meae,* could
you have confessed to me so casually that you found your
interest in Blake waning? You still *perceive* his excellence,
you tell me, but it no longer matters whether he is excellent

or not. Has he himself not obliquely refuted you when, in his *Marriage of Heaven and Hell,* he reminds us: "Truth can never be told so as to be understood, and not be believ'd"? If his excellence has ceased to matter, then you have ceased to perceive it—and where am I to turn, who realize only too well that the very foundations of our union rest upon Blake? If there was one event of great import in my life, it was the day in Altmann's meadow when we read *The Everlasting Gospel,* with its sublime doggerel so helpful to us in our uncertainties at that time. For it enwrapped our humble desires in a gorgeous vocabulary, making us feel that not merely you and I, but all Mankind and Womanhood, were on that day approaching each other. We were encouraged to scorn a law "writ with Curses from Pole to Pole," were told that God himself is no more than man, and that "Mary was found in Adulterous bed."

> "But this, O Lord, this was my Sin
> When first I let these devils in:
> In dark pretence to Chastity
> Blaspheming Love, blaspheming thee."

You, to my astonishment, paused to repeat these lines. I was terrified at your sudden lewd promise, stated thus with the authority of a great poet, and I myself begged you to put me away until I should make myself more worthy of you.

So consider, my dear, how much you would take from us by this moody heresy. Let us admit no "idiot Questioner" in matters of such great moment to our relationship. And you should not protest at my homage. How could you in any way feel yourself "absurd" when I write you as I do? You should find it only natural that I praise you diligently; you should receive me amply, and think no further.

Yet I have been more disciplined than you would suspect. I have spared you all the letters I wrote you following the announcement of your delay. I had bought tickets for the opera, which I could ill afford; but that I might not be there wholly without you, I did not turn back the ticket to the seat which you would have occupied. Thus by my subterfuge, in your very absence you were somehow with me. "The weak in courage is strong in cunning"—and I have contrived many tricks of thinking to help bear me up.

How pleasant, after the strained hours I had spent recently in the coercing of my story, to place myself at the disposal of a master, to let him dictate when there should be risings and when subsidences. I assisted him—and together we mounted to assertion, capped by kettledrums. And as another evidence of my cunning, I left the theatre before the close of the performance, I went away while the violins were repeating a design in unison, ever more softly, and the stage gradually darkened, suggesting the submerged castle of a fish bowl and the mighty distances discoverable there by peering. I left before the end that I might carry away the sense of the opera's continuing—and for several hours afterwards it seemed as though the vast battle were still in progress. I went from opera sounds to street sounds, but the imperiousness of the music was still strong in me, and every casual noise was translated into the perfect note most like it. Thus the discordant city sang melodically and contrapuntally. Were I a charitable deity, looking down upon what was there myself, if I were such a deity, observing that hollow replica, and concerned with nothing but his particular respite, I should have said: "Strike him down—let him at this moment cease." And if there is disloyalty to you in such a thought, take it as the one sign I will give you of my discouragement at your delay. Oh, I am tired—tired of trying to deserve you, tired of writing you so constantly and so unmanfully. May you come soon, to repair all this—may you come, that I may nestle against you, and repeat then with comfort:

"Ah! gentle may I lay me down and gentle rest my head,
And gentle sleep the sleep of death, and gentle hear the voice
Of him that walketh in the garden in the evening time."

Jan. 19

Please do not hold it against me that I was so long in answering you. You will understand me when I say that I had to wait for a little competence. I had to find such a way of writing you that I should not pain you either by vindictiveness or by too greatly appealing to your pity. I could not write to wish you well until not only my words, but the man writing these words in his empty room, could wish you well. And in all fairness, I must agree with you as to the wisdom of your choice. I did not hold out a very encouraging future to you.

"Damn braces. Bless relaxes." Yet I will not equip myself against you by venom. I will tell myself always that you were sweet, and thus I shall remain unfortified. For if I hated you now, how could I continue to love you in the past—and for me not to love you in the past would be an impoverishment beyond endurance. Oh yes, I will not deny that for some weeks the Undersigned has been a "Male Form howling in Jealousy," his Emanation torn from him. He "furious refuses to repose." He has the disconcerting documents at his fingertips, recalls that "the nakedness of woman is the work of God," that "Women, the comforters of Men, become their Tormentors & Punishers," nor can he dismiss the recollection of a lovely twilight when, after the two of them had walked for many miles, and had eaten the supper he carried in his knapsack, they nestled together under birch trees. He needs but imagine another in his place, and the picture is circumstantial enough. "Dip him in the river who loves water." Yet not Blake, but you, have taught me not to invite disaster.

"The Hermaphroditic Condensations are divided by the Knife,
The obdurate Forms are cut asunder by Jealousy and Pity."

Of jealousy I have spoken. I know that in jealousy the world is lost. Yet jealousy is but incidental to deep single love; it is the risk, not the essence; and if the world is lost in jealousy, in deep single love the world may be well lost. The possibilities of delight were worth the eventualities of torture. As for pity, though there is a division in pity, and though I had sworn not to ask for pity, I shall be content with pity. I shall tell myself that you have not ceased to worry for me. Thus

I shall relinquish a great deal that I may salvage a little, for one should not try to save too much in a fire. Oh, I am caught in the "mind-forg'd manacles," though in this case they are not the manacles of reason, but the manacles of a relentless, unreasoning memory.

I know of a man who, in a moment of blind self-interest that undid its own purposes, had sent away a lovely woman. Needing money, he had suggested sullenly that she procure some as best she was able, yet there had been much delicacy in his possession of her. She left the room without reproaching him, but he never saw her again thereafter—and with each succeeding month he understood more bitterly the destitution he had brought upon himself. He found that she alone had upheld him, for there was no pliancy in him that had not come from sources within this woman. He remembered how they had crept together, with the city roaring about them like a monster; how he had felt the warmth of her while she slept, as though they alone were spared from a cataclysm, as though all mankind, torn by madness, were fleeing from danger, while they lay safely in sweet segregation, enclosed in the Ark of their four walls, and the torrents of the metropolis pounded outside their windows. But the room had since become barren of her—so he grew humble, he grew really pitiable, and I was very sorry for him, particularly as I saw a feeling of strangeness and loneliness come over him, and I knew that by his very need of companionship he drove people from him. There seemed no way of rescuing him, for if some one spoke to him easily, he would promptly whisper to himself, "See, the man felt no strain in addressing me," and in thinking such thoughts he would betray them to the speaker, who then felt uneasy, and shied away at an excessive leaping-up of gladness. Let us hope, my dear, that I do not, in my own way, gradually lapse into this man's strangeness—but I fear lest all that smiled readily in me has been taken from me.

I enclose, along with my felicitations, my unfinished manuscript. What cause could I have to plague myself with it further? It was meant purely to earn me certain privileges

which are no longer available. With this I say good-bye. And
that you may not think me wholly alone, I say good-by also
in behalf of the wooden policeman, who must know something
about you since he has stared his paint-stare directly into my
eyes. I shall write you no further. I have not the slightest
notion what I shall do next. I shall vaguely advance—and
perhaps, by the subterfuges of the cowardly cunning, I shall
have nothing more real than the wooden man for my grotesque
crony, as I go towards the tangled and uncharted, into

> "Realms
> Of terror & mild moony lustre, in soft sexual delusions
> Of varied beauty to delight the wanderer and repose
> His burning thirst and freezing hunger!"

Henceforth I shall at best be one of those "that live a
pestilence and die a meteor and are no more."

                                                   March 8

To my dear dead Mistress,
    I did, it is true, promise never to write you again. But surely
you will allow me the harmless pleasure of a make-believe
correspondence, writing letters you never receive, and answering letters you never sent.
    Well, it has not been so painful as I had feared, this being
deprived of Emanation, and cursed by Selfhood. With the
unfinished manuscript I sent you, the bafflements of fiction
have ceased, and now I roam about devoid of any such grave
responsibilities. One tramps streets of dirty, half-melted snow,
observing the minor incidents of traffic. In sitting among
audiences, and looking in the same direction with them, one
feels not wholly outcast. I read but seldom, even Blake I read
but seldom. The Ariel-like songs run through my head occasionally, but I am not, at this time, so greatly attracted to his
mythological pieces, with their clangorous forge-music, "ut-
tered with Hammer & Anvil," their cosmic lamentations, their
accounts of vast Beings' wombs raped vastly, their torrents,

violent awakings, earthquakes, rebirths. Such fountainheads of poetry are not wholly germane to my chief problems at present.

I have heard of people who found it impossible to prevent themselves from counting numbers, and continued long into the night, in anguish, piling up their involuntary sums. Similarly with me, the idea of the dummy policeman has come to be troublesome. Perhaps I should take a room in some other section of the city. For this absurd figure stands too prominently in my path. With a life so uneventful as mine, it becomes too much of an event for me to pass him. And even while sitting in my room, as let us say on some snowy night when I have no intention of going out, I keep thinking of him on the street below, with stolidly upraised hand, the sleet curving about his pedestal. There is nothing particularly unpleasant in the thought of him except its constancy. And I can assure you: he is so unchanging, that to think of him repeatedly is to feel the mind inexorably rigid. To consider him against one's wishes is like maintaining a constant muscular tension. So you may, before long, find me in retreat from this grotesque danger. If he continues to claim more of my attention, I shall certainly take a room in another section of the city.

March 28

My dear dead Mistress,

One reason the figure has taken such a hold upon me is that I have had little opportunity to bury its effects beneath more natural kinds of relationship. Seeing a child in a carriage, I took advantage of its ignorance to wheedle a smile from it— and the mother came near me hurriedly, meaning no insult, but clearly nervous at finding me so close to something she thought precious. A sweet woman once took delight in the touch of me, and I sat in many ordinary places conversing with strangers readily enough, and people did not think it odd—but now I can approach no human thing without remarkableness.

Two young men recently sat on the same bench with me in the park. They seemed like students, and from their conversation I knew that their studies were of great import to them. Thus I felt I could tell them things which might somewhat engross them; but when I spoke, though I quoted good authors in order to make my equipment apparent to them in my opening sentences, they showed clearly that they resented my intrusion. The far one uncrossed his legs, so I knew that the boys would leave me as soon as possible. I talked hastily to them about the vicious circle, calling it both "vicious circle" and *circulus vitiosus,* using the Latin that they might know me for no ordinary man on a park bench, and the English lest they might not understand the Latin. "I am in a vicious circle," I said in haste, for they were growing shifty. There are accounts of such vicious circles in folklore, I explained to them, as stories of a once handsome prince locked up in a repellent form. "These are stories of the vicious circle," I told them, "for the Prince will not be freed until the love of a beautiful woman has freed him—and how, short of magic, can a beautiful woman love him until his true form is revealed?" But I had made them very uncomfortable, so I turned abruptly and went away from them. Surely they smiled to each other behind my back; yet had they made friends with me simply as an oddity, and admitted me into their lives on any terms, if only as a king might keep a dwarf or a parrot, I should gradually have been reclaimed. Of this I am certain.

April 3

My dear dead Mistress,

I am a little frightened today, for the rigidity of my existence is unquestionably beginning to tell against me. If one were to make his hand into a fist so tightly clenched that the whole arm trembled, and were to translate this feeling to mental things, he could imagine somewhat how my mind is. It is as though my mind had muscles, and these muscles would not relax. The steadiness of my preoccupation causes this feeling of muscles under tension. It is as though the pulpy substance of the brain were turning into muscle, and these muscles were straining to tear apart their own tissues. This feeling is clearly the result of a tension caused by a changeless image which I cannot dismiss. But just as the eye accommodates itself to blinding lights, or the skin gradually learns to withstand heat of great intensity, I could probably make myself sufficiently at home under this discipline, did I not have a fear that its severity is growing. I had become competent enough—but today, when I passed my policeman, a quick impulse seized me, and before I knew what I was doing, I had spoken to the policeman. I wish I had not done this—and I should not have done it had I been aware of the temptation in advance. Just as though he were alive, I smiled at him and spoke. I was passing directly in front of him when, to my astonishment, I heard myself saying, "Hello, Joe." I could have done the same under happier circumstances, but the meaning would not have been the same. It is quite natural to address inanimate things—it is no more foolish than confiding secrets to a dog. But as I looked about apprehensively, I saw that a woman had observed me. She was pretty, and insolent, and was watching me intently. There was no kindness in her eyes, nothing but cold curiosity. Her eyes, my dear, passed a terrible judgment upon me. And to escape her judgment, I repeated my greeting, this time leaning back, squinting, and waving my hand, as though I had been speaking to some one in the recesses of the store—but now I noticed that the clerk inside, with a bewildered moonface, was staring at me glumly. I am now bending beneath eyes, the wooden eyes of the policeman, the cold curious eyes of the woman, and the glum eyes of the clerk inside the store.

April 7

To my dear, dead Mistress,
     My life is a funnel—and with each day I am squeezed

farther into its narrow end. This morning, with a strange assurance, I leapt from my bed, dressed, and hurried down to
the street, just that I might pass the policeman and show myself that I could pass him without speaking. I did pass him
without speaking, without even a desire to speak to him. But
when I had returned to my room, a voice said to me, "Could
you pass him again without speaking?" So I went down and
passed him again. Five times today I have passed the policeman, to convince myself that I need not speak to him as I
pass him; but each time, as I go back to my room, the doubt
returns.

Now, it has occurred to me, why should I not speak to the
policeman? I have been plagued by the conviction that I
should not speak to him—and the obvious way of overcoming
that is to let oneself speak to him. I had made a new temptation by making a new crime—and I shall remove them both at
once. Hereafter, if I happen to desire to address the dummy,
I shall do so. I shall speak to him as often as I please. And
as a precaution against cold curious stares of unsympathetic
women, I shall speak to him covertly, from the corner of my
mouth, behind my handkerchief, or by hiding my mouth with
my hand as though I were scratching my nose.

Memorandum: Rules to Self: If a person whistles or calls, give
no evidence of hearing. The signal was not intended for you. If
children begin shouting, do not quicken your pace. The shouting has to do with some game of theirs. You are dressed like
every other man that passes along these streets. If strangers
in the city stop to ask you directions, act as though you spoke
another language and did not understand them. You know
by now that when they ask you questions, your knowledge
of the commonest streets will vanish from your memory. So
avoid embarrassment by acting as though you could not understand them. Never stop beside some one who is looking
in a shop window, if he is alone. For you know how it irritates
you when you are standing alone looking in a shop window
and some one stops beside you and begins looking at the same

things. If you decide to go the other way, try to remember not to turn suddenly—for likely as not there will be some one behind you, and his face will be thrust directly into yours.

April 8

My dear Mistress,

No, you are not dead. Praise God, you are not dead. When I finally need to do so, I can really write to you, can actually mail one of these letters to you. So you may soon be hearing from me in reality, for I may need your help, I may have to call upon you to end a certain process. Today it seemed that the policeman actually acknowledged me in passing. I know that the policeman did not speak to me. It was probably some chance street-sound that was interpreted, by my tired body, as a voice coming from him. And it was probably a mere quiver of my eyelids which made me imagine for a moment that his lips moved. Besides, any rigid thing, if watched intently, will seem to stir. Who has not, on observing a statue or a corpse, seen the breast heave in respiration? When the dummy seemed to stir for a moment I was not frightened. But a second later, apprehension came over me. I looked about—and as I had feared, the cold curious woman was eyeing me, and passing the same judgment upon me. Oh, I am very tired. I should like to fall into a deep sleep, and on awaking, find every single thing around me altogether different.

I said that I could write you? On the contrary, I must not think of writing you. Probably it was the weakness of these make-believe letters that first started me on my course into the funnel. I must put myself under severer rules. I must deny myself all these little subterfuges which pamper me. This the last word that passes between us.

From *Towards a Better Life: A Series of Declamations or Epistles* (New York: Harcourt, Brace, 1932), pp. 171-194.

The Range of Piety
(*1935*)

Magical and Utilitarian Meanings

One cannot long discuss the question of meaning, as applied to the field of art, without coming upon the problem of piety. Santayana has somewhere defined piety as loyalty to the sources of our being. Such a notion should suggest that piety is not confined to the strictly religious sphere. It would as well be present when the potter molds the clay to exactly that form which completely gratifies his sense of how it ought to be. The connection between our pieties and our childhood should seem clear, since in childhood we develop our first patterns of judgment, while the experiences of maturity are revisions and amplifications of these childhood patterns. An adult, for instance, may turn his thoughts from a father to a father-government; yet even in later life, should he take an axe and fell a great tree, we need not be surprised to find a strange misgiving permeate him as the noble symbol of shelter comes crashing to the earth. For however neutral his act, though the tree had been felled to satisfy the simple utilitarian needs of firewood, there may also be lurking here a kind of symbolic parricide. Not only firewood, but a parent-symbol, may be brought down in the crash.

It is possible that much of the anguish affecting poets in the modern world is due to the many symbolic outrages which a purely utilitarian philosophy of action requires us to commit. In primitive eras, when the utilitarian processes were considerably fewer, and more common to the entire group, definite propitiatory rituals seem to have arisen as a way of canceling off these symbolic offenses. In the magical orientation (so close to that of poetry) if the felling of a tree had connotations of symbolic parricide, the group would probably develop a corresponding ritual of symbolic expiation. The offender

48

would thus have a technique for cleansing himself of the sin he had committed.

The purely utilitarian attitude towards such acts, however, requires that one introduce a distinctly impious note: one cannot permit the symbolic overtones of meaning to function at all. If the tree falls, and one feels a strange uneasiness, one must shut off the queer remorse by an impatient "Nonsense!—this is only one tree, I needed it, and there are plenty of others to take its place." The nonutilitarian qualities of the act are dismissed—one must perform the act as a "new man"—and when a great oak falls, only the poet, bewildered and plaintive, may permit himself to feel that there is somehow a deeper issue here than the mere getting of firewood. (Whereat, thinking of modern "negativistic" trends, we might contrast "Woodman, spare that tree . . ." with the dictum of a contemporary poet who defined style imagistically as the resonance of the axe in the wood.)

Such considerations may be at the bottom of the tendency, often noted in esthetic theory, to stress a direct antithesis between artistic and practical responses. For if our speculations are correct, it would follow that the purely utilitarian attitude could be upheld only by the suppression of those very overtones to which the earnest poet most resolutely exposes himself. And we may see why a writer of so deeply poetic a nature as Nietzsche felt that the purely rationalistic, utilitarian ideal required the perfection of a different breed, a superman who would be hard and brutal in the performance of his acts.

Perhaps an instance of the way in which the rational, scientific categories of linkage can run counter to the emotional categories may be seen in the classifying of the lion. The lion, if the usual psychoanalytic theory of symbolization is correct, is the male or father symbol *par excellence.* Yet the lion is scientifically included in the cat family, whereas the cat emotionally is feminine. In both great poetry and popular usage, it is associated with female attributes. Here we have, in our rational categories, an association which runs entirely counter to the associations of our emotional categories. A linkage emotionally appropriate becomes rationally inappropriate.

In such cases, where the rational order of symbols would establish a congruity wholly alien to the emotional order of symbols, is it not possible that intense conflicts could arise, with the result that anguish or unrest could follow any really thorough attempt to embrace the rational category? And might we see in Darwin's intense attacks of vertigo an evidence of precisely such a conflict? For Darwin furnishes the supreme instance of the tendency to construct rational categories which are at variance with the categories of linkage formed in emotional experience. His transference of man from the category of the divine to the category of the apes is, as the popular resistance to his new categories testified, the most obvious instance, though the same affront runs through the entire schema of biological classifications, as distinct from the linkages of the emotions. It is even recorded that women fainted when first being told of his conclusions (possibly because of the disturbing implication that they had been sleeping with apes). And for my own part, I shall never forget my great resentment as a child upon learning that lions were cats, whereas to me they were purely and simple the biggest dogs.

No wonder an intensity of purely illogical Symbolist linkages broke out in poetry precisely at the time when the rational schema of classification had come into full flower. Poets, whose logic is rooted in experience, were now faced with a contrary logic wholly the product of rational speculation, and their bewilderment was considerable. The fertilizer company has a much different attitude towards a dead dog than does the child who may have had it for a pet. The child's kind of linkage could be called poetic or magical, in contrast with the utilitarian linkage of the chemical concern. It would be pious of a man to accept the full childhood implications of his adult performances, to take fully into account the need of expiation in case the tree which he was felling happened to be a parent-symbol as well as an aggregate of firewood. And much of the criminality in modern life might be explained psychologically as due to the loss of a definite, generally recognized technique for canceling off these hidden offenses. Justification by success must replace the deeper-lying kind of magical justification—and since such success usually involves the strengthening of one's skill in precisely the act which contains the symbolic affront, the test of success must in time inure one to his role as malefactor. Such a possibility might lead us to look for equally devious modes of expiation among the practical-minded.

In any case, if piety is the sort of response we have described, it would seem to possess the following notable features: (1) It would show a marked affinity with childhood experiences, thus explaining, among other things, why poets living in a period of great change so often tend to become infantile. For it would suggest the deep connection between piety and the "remembrance of things past." (2) It would suggest why piety can be painful, requiring a set of symbolic expiations (such as martyrdom or intense ambition) to counteract the symbolic offenses involved in purely utilitarian actions.

Piety as a System-Builder

Furthermore, piety is a system-builder, a desire to round things out, to fit experiences together into a unified whole. Piety is *the sense of what properly goes with what.* And it leads to construction in this way: If there is an altar, it is pious of man to perform some ritual act whereby he may approach this altar with clean hands. A kind of symbolic cleanliness goes with altars, a technique of symbolic cleansing goes with cleanliness, a preparation or initiation goes with the technique of cleansing, the need of cleansing was based upon some feeling of taboo—and so on, until pious linkages may have brought all the significant details of the day into coordination, relating them integrally with one another by a complex interpretative network.

If it is pious to exemplify a sense of the appropriate, there must be other aspects of piety not generally called such. Besides the pieties of love (birds and flowers for one's mistress— or the Elizabethan's promptness in getting from thoughts of young female beauty to the themes of honor and of *carpe diem*), there would be the less devout appropriatenesses of art: thus the villain of a bad drama speaks in sibilants; or a symphony, at an heroic moment, blares with its brasses; or the poet, writing of night, puts together all those elements that are his night-thoughts, the things that go with night as he knows it, and perhaps lying in his Paris room, he hears outside, lone crabs scraping on the street.

I would even go further in trying to establish this notion of piety as a response which extends through all the texture of our lives but has been concealed from us because we think we are so thoroughly without religion and think that the "pious process" is confined to the sphere of churchliness. Bentham discovered that poetry (a *poor* brand of poetry) is implicit in our very speech. For our words affect us and our hearers by drawing upon the wells of emotion behind them. We cannot speak the mother-tongue without employing the rhetorical devices of a Roman orator. And Bentham saw in the neutral vocabularies of science an attempt to eliminate this unconscious piety from speech. (He did not go on to ask whether this whole desire for a neutral vocabulary might be interpreted as one vast castration-symbol suspiciously expiatory in essence, particularly in the case of this crotchety old bachelor who formulated his neutral ideal with such avidity, though such an ingredient would be more likely discoverable in a messianic temperament like Bentham than in the ordinary run of his followers.) So if we are all poets, and if all poets are pious, we may expect to find great areas of piety, even at a ball game. Indeed, all life has been likened to the writing of a poem, though some people write their poems on paper, and others carve theirs out of jugular veins.

As I call piety merely the sense of what goes with what, I have opened myself to a *reductio ad absurdum*, thus: Suppose there is a flock of birds and that one of them, rightly or wrongly, is frightened into flight; the rest of the flock rises also. In other words, the flight of the flock goes with the flight of the one. By our definition, this gregarious obedience would be piety.

Piety is a schema of orientation, since it involves the putting together of experiences. The orientation may be right or wrong; it can guide or misguide. If the bird saw an actual danger, the flock was right in rising with it. If the danger was not real, the flock was wrong. In either case it had been pious.

Extending our term still further: If one is long unhappy, and living alone with his unhappiness (as wounded animals slink off by themselves to die), and if he hears next door, at a certain hour each day, a peculiar nagging way of a doorbell's ringing, he may even come to link the significance of his distress with the significance of this doorbell. He will connect his outstanding misery with the outstanding nature of the sound—and years later, should he survive his misery, and be quite tough again, he may one day hear a bell ring next door, in a peculiarly nagging way, whereat an unspeakable heaviness will fall upon him. In this linkage, an outlaw appropriateness decidedly "Proustian," he will have committed a piety. Such are the pieties of moodiness, merging into insanity.

We are now prepared to carry our term to its limit. Refined critics, of the Matthew Arnold variety, assumed that exquisiteness of taste was restricted to the "better" classes of people, those who never had names ending in "ug." Yet if we can bring ourselves to imagine Matthew Arnold loafing on the corner with the gashouse gang, we promptly realize how undiscriminating he would prove himself. Everything about him would be inappropriate: both what he said and the ways in which he said it. Consider the crudeness of his perception as regards the proper oaths, the correct way of commenting upon passing women, the etiquette of spitting. Does not his very crassness here reveal the presence of a morality, a deeply felt and piously obeyed sense of the appropriate, on the part

of these men, whose linkages he would outrageously violate?
Watch them—and observe with what earnestness, what *devotion,* these gashouse Matthew Arnolds act to prove themselves,
every minute of the day, true members of their cult. Vulgar-
ity is pious.

These considerations force us to reinterpret what jurists or
social workers often look upon as decay, degeneracy, disintegration, and the like. If a man who is a criminal lets the
criminal trait in him serve as the informing aspect of his
character, piously taking unto him all other traits and habits
that he feels should go with his criminality, the criminal
deterioration which the moralist with another point of view
might discover in him is the very opposite of deterioration as
regards the tests of piety. It is *integration,* guided by a scrupulous sense of the appropriate which, once we dismiss our
personal locus of judgment, would seem to bear the marks of
great conscientiousness.

Similarly with the "drug fiend," who can take his morphine
in a hospital without the slightest disaster to his character,
since it is called medicine there; but if he injects it at a party,
where it has the stigma of dissipation upon it, he may gradually organize his character about this outstanding "altar" of his
experience—and since the altar in this case is generally accepted as unclean, he will be disciplined enough to approach
it with appropriately unclean hands, until he is a derelict.
Like Holmes's chambered nautilus, which was always held
up to us in our school days as an example of sound development, he will add one cell upon another, constructing an
integer of wickedness out of deference to the norms of his
times. He puts himself together by the social recipes all about
him, his so-called decay being marked by as scrupulous and
discerning a selectivity as in a poem by Keats.

There is, of course, a further factor involved here: the matter of *interaction.* Certain of one's choices become creative in
themselves; they drive one into ruts, and these ruts in turn
reenforce one's piety. Once one has jumped over a cliff, for
instance, he can let events take care of themslves, confident in

the knowledge that he will continue to maintain and intensify his character as one-who-has-jumped-over-a-cliff. To translate: Should a man given to crime or drugs become discouraged by the risks or distresses caused by his transgression, he might feel strong inducements towards apostasy. The altar of criminality or drug addiction might prove too exacting, so that he desired to reconstruct his linkages with some other less troublesome altar as the informing principle of his character.

Yet he may already have gone so far that other people are also helping him to continue in the same direction. He has become hypnotically entangled in the texture of his poem, as objectified in the external relationships he has already established. He can no longer retract his vow—hence, he is spared the trivial lapses that might otherwise have interrupted his devotion to the character of his offense; at times of weakness and doubt, when his own convictions are not enough to sustain him, he is kept under discipline by the walls of his monastery (that is, by the ruts which his experience itself has worn).

From *Permanence and Change: An Anatomy of Purpose* (2nd ed.; Los Altos, Calif.: Hermes Publications, 1954), pp. 71-79.

Secular Conversions

(*1935*)

The Fundamentals of Psychoanalysis

In closing this section, perhaps we should study that region in which *interpretation* and *therapy* most clearly converge: those secular bringers of good tidings, the psychoanalysts. From our standpoint, psychoanalysis can be treated as a simple technique of nonreligious conversion. It effects its cures by providing a new perspective that dissolves the system of pieties lying at the roots of the patient's sorrows or bewilderments. It is an *impious* rationalization, offering a fresh terminology of motives to replace the patient's painful terminology of motives. Its scientific terms are wholly incongruous with the unscientific nature of the distress. By approaching the altar of the patient's unhappiness with deliberate irreverence, by selecting a vocabulary which specifically violates the dictates of style and taboo, it changes the entire nature of his problem, rephrasing it in a form for which there is a solution. Insofar as it is curative, its effects seem due to the fact that it exorcises the painful influences of a vestigial religious orientation by appeal to the prestige of the newer scientific orientation.

Even so virtuous a faith as Christianity situated the crux of conversion, not in *goodness*, but in *belief*. So we need not be surprised to find evidence that, in the secular rebirth engineered by the psychoanalytic seer, the processes of recovery from one's effective disorders are closely interwoven with a shifting of one's intellectualistic convictions, one's terminology of cause, purpose, and prophecy. *Theory* (literally, a *looking-at*, or *viewing*) plays a large part, not only in the technique of the physician, but in the patient's response. Psychonalysis may be described as a new rationalization, offered to the patient in place of an older one which had got him into difficulties. The patient, with pious devotion, had erected a consistent network of appropriatenesses about the altar of his wretchedness, the thoroughness of the outlying structure thus tending to maintain the integrity of the basic psychosis. Yet the discomfiture itself laid him open *to the need of new meanings,* hence offering the psychoanalyst a grip within the terms of the psychosis itself. For one can cure a psychosis only by appealing to some aspect of the psychosis. The cure must bear notable affinities with the disease: all effective medicines are potential poisons.

Freud's great informing invention for the recommending of a kindlier, more Christian rationalization to replace the angry Jehovah of the earlier schemes was his doctrine of the six abnormal tendencies. These served as a remarkably accurate formulation for that kind of perspective by incongruity which we might call the opposite of magnification: conversion downwards—reduction of scale. The working of this device as a conversion *downwards* was really paradoxical—for on the face of it the device was of exactly the opposite sort. It seemed to be a universal slander, rather than a mitigating principle, for it said that *everyman* was in essence a pervert. Everyman, Freud assured his patients, had in him, and in the symbolism of his thoughts, speech, and actions, the six abnormal tendencies: autoeroticism, homosexuality, sadism, masochism, incest, and exhibitionism.

There were two extremely valuable aspects of this formula. In the first place, it is hard to imagine a single manifestation of human interests which could not be reduced to one of these six terms. A heterosexual interest, for instance, could be sadistic or masochistic, even down to the last subtle give-and-take of conversational repartee. And if one, at such a juncture, attempted to prove himself neither sadistic nor masochistic, by refraining from a retort of any kind, he was obviously open to the suspicion of an incipient autoeroticism, or perhaps a twisted kind of exhibitionism manifesting itself by blatant noncooperation, or perhaps even a silently corroding incestuousness which was dragging his mind elsewhere. One can invent hypothetical cases at random, noting that the "six abnormals" will serve as well as any other terms to designate the underlying patterns of the mind. Such comprehensiveness of terminology, while offered under the guise of great specificity, had the signal virtue of catching all conduct in its net. Even a man who had been wholly bewildered by the "irrationality" of his conduct was given a scheme of motivations which promptly brought him back into the realm of "logic."

This gets us to the second great virtue of Freud's formula as regards the therapeutics of suggestion. If the six abnormals applied to everybody, it followed that everybody was abnormal, hence it followed that it was normal to be abnormal. Thus, as Marston has observed, the doctrine of the six abnormals seems to have rediscovered, under a technical or clinical terminology more in keeping with the antireligious temper of the century, the old Church doctrine of original sin, which had long proved its curative value during the heyday of the Catholic rationalization. In a great century of progress based upon the doctrine of the innate goodness of man, or of his perfectibility through evolution, Freud reformulated the old doctrine of original sin to cure the people whom progress, in some form or another, was driving into hysteria. The pansexuality of Freud's formulae seems to have been especially effective because sexual emphases were already outstanding in the orientation of his day, hence a sexual symptom could most easily recommend itself as the *core* of the entire situation, with all else as mere incidental by-products.

It is not our purpose here to refute Freudian theory or to choose among the various schools of thought that have descended from it. We are interested simply in pointing out certain notable features of the conversion technique which seem to characterize them all. These are primarily of two sorts: the *conversion downwards* of the patient's distress by means of an unfit, incongruous terminology—and the positive development of a substitute terminology until it has provided the patient with a brand-new rationalization of motives.

As regards the first point, the procedure that most obviously serves the ends of impiety is that of sitting down and talking the matter over—and every school of analysis seems to stress the therapeutic value of this clinic-confessional. Freud, Adler, Jung, Rivers, and McDougall have all, within the terms of their systems, found explanations for the necessity and efficacy of this practice. Essentially, it is at the very roots of incongruity, bringing a professional, dispassionate, detached point of view to bear upon a subject matter which has been surrounded with the pieties of intense personal devotion, awe, and silence (and authors, as well as mystics, have testified to the accumulative power of silence).

It has been laid against Hegel that he tended to solve old riddles of philosophy by simply redefining them, by approaching them in different terms, so that the earlier issues were not so much *solved* as *dissolved*. History itself has a way of doing likewise, letting old battlefields merge into a single spot as the rise of other interests takes us remotely elsewhere—and likewise many private difficulties are better handled by an *integral neglect* than by a direct attempt at reconciliation. I do not mean that they are *suppressed*, I mean that they are *allowed to languish*—and nothing is more destructive of beauties rising before bowed head and silence than a competent, professional air, at once sympathetic with the problem and unimpressed with its gravity.

Here is a fundamental incongruity, or impiety, proper to all psychiatric methods—and often, as a matter of fact, the pious sufferer resists it as such. Thus Freud mentions frequent violent antagonism on the part of the patient, Adler stoically asserts that the analyst may even have to accept physical blows as his reward for this impious affront upon the patient's sorrowful poem. For we must expect to meet with fury, when desecrating the altar of a patient's misery, to which he has brought the most pious offerings, weaving about it the very texture of his self-respect, developing an entire schema of motivations above this central orientating concern, profoundly stressing certain values and rejecting others according to their fitness for this integrative work, and clinging to the structure all the more passionately since, if it began as the *cause* of his distress, by the time the patient has finished building, it has become his only bulwark against distress.

McDougall's Modifications of Freudianism

In his *Outline of Abnormal Psychology*, McDougall specifically disapproves of Freud's approach on the grounds that Freud's terms omit precisely the factor in mental unbalance which McDougall considers the most important of all: dissociation. McDougall finds it remarkable that, whereas authorities like Janet and Morton Prince regard dissociation as the most important and far-reaching explanatory principle to be applied in interpreting neurotic disorder, Freud makes no use of this conception. He says that to his knowledge the word does not even appear in any of Freud's principle writings.

McDougall's theory is based entirely upon the stressing of this omitted concept. Like his fellow countryman, the neurologist Sherrington, he stresses the need of integration, by which he means a single guiding principle, or purpose, which can coordinate tendencies more or less at odds with one another. He calls these minor conflicting tendencies "monads," after Leibniz, though seeming to differ from Leibniz' use of the term in the sense that there is not a pre-established harmony among them. According to McDougall, in fact, sane mental adjustment requires the *forcible* establishment of such a harmony. The minor monads are compelled to obey a *monas monadum,* which is the "self-regarding principle." This self-regarding principle, or "master principle," is the all-embracing personality which forces the various conflicting sub-personalities into line.

As an illustration of integration, McDougall uses the example of the British Empire, and as an illustration of the dissociative tendency, he cites the rebelliousness of Ireland. He thinks that the key to the problems of individual psychology is to be found in cases of multiple personality, in which some aspects of the individual so sharply conflict with others that they make different personality systems, and may even be felt by the sufferer as different selves. He cites various instances of split personality, most notably Dr. Morton Prince's famous case of Miss Beauchamp. His notion is that we are all examples of divided personality, that different degrees of hypnosis can serve to bring out one or another of our personality-systems, and that the content of our dreams reveals the workings of these other personalities even in normal people, while the breaks in the continuity of dreams may represent transitions from one personality to another.

All these sub-personalities are held together under normal conditions by an ideal personality, which coordinates the others in accordance with its supreme demands, as shaped by the self-regarding principle. But in times of stress or exhaustion, some of the submerged personalities may take the opportunity to exert themselves with extreme vigor, sometimes causing such marked division of personality that a sufferer has even been known to read a page as two selves, with one of his selves reading faster than the other, and reaching the bottom of the page before it. Thus may the personalities conflict, he says, quite as Ireland, always fuming under suppression, took advantage of the Empire's distresses in World War I to proclaim a distinct personality and demand autonomy.

McDougall cites this merely to illustrate his theory of motivations—yet might it not partially have instigated his framing of the theory itself? And might this very analogy with the Empire's political patterns make it more useful as a cure for specifically British sufferers? For if the individual's scheme of motives is but one aspect of a larger interpretative frame, it would be natural that the perplexities of an Englishman should be normalized or socialized by reference to meanings involved in the structure of the Empire as a whole. In offering the patient a theory of motives molded after the Empire, is he not reclaiming individual orientation by linking it with the general political orientation, thereby connecting the private pieties with the social pieties?

Note how he further exemplifies this "imperialist" sense of order when, under the heading, "The Appeal to Sentiments," he warns that the bringer of new meanings should not attempt "conversion" in the absolute sense which Nietzsche had in mind, a revaluation of *all* values, but should appeal to any normal standards which the patient still held intact. The physician is warned not to attempt a radical remaking of his patient, but to get whatever toehold he can upon the patient's past dispositions, not obliterating old systems entirely, but taking them over in sound imperialistic fashion and making them serve the purpose of the new order which he would impose upon them.

Poor Nietzsche, with his German *Gründlichkeit,* which

either dominates or collapses, proposing to change everything *von Haus aus:* how different his scheme of conversion from that advocated by this diplomatic Britisher, who would "muddle through" the processes of cure! We do not make this point to cast aspersions upon Professor McDougall's theories. On the contrary, we are trying to suggest why these theories might be expected to have genuine curative effects. For in rebuilding the "master personality" along the lines of the nation's political pattern, he is socializing the patient's new mental structure by anchoring it to an obvious feature of the *group psychosis.*

As evidence that our suggestion is not excessive we recall in Professor Dewey's *Art as Experience* a discussion of the way in which our psychological vocabulary originated. He says that the words for describing the pattern of the mind were borrowed by analogy from the patterns of the state. "They were at first formulations of differences found among the portions and classes of society." He cites Plato as a perfect instance of this, saying that Plato openly borrowed his three-fold division of the soul from the situation which he observed in the communal life of the times. He observes that Plato is here doing consciously what many a psychologist has since done unconsciously, who divides up the mind in accordance with differences observable in the society about him while thinking that he has arrived at them by pure introspection. Plato, says Professor Dewey, formulated the sensuously acquisitive portion of the mind after the analogy of the mercantile class, his picture of the "spirited" faculty corresponded to the citizen-soldiers, while the "reason" was patterned after the group empowered to make the laws.

Our point of view should also explain why even a factor which McDougall considers so all-important as dissociation can be omitted entirely from a theory of human motivation without destroying the possibilities of cure. Freud wrote for a people who had, for many centuries, accommodated themselves to imperial decay—perhaps he wrote for something which we might call the "psychosis of the Strauss waltz."

Hence, his devices for reorientation would be differently framed, to correspond with differences in the local orientation of his group.

Exorcism by Misnomer

Why is it so necessary that the patient be told the nature and origin of his disorder? Does one truly cast out devils by *naming* them? The notion of perspective by incongruity would suggest that one casts out devils by *misnaming* them. It is not the *naming* in itself that does the work, but the *conversion downward* implicit in such naming. Has one seen a child trembling in terror at a vague shape in a corner? One goes impiously into the corner, while the child looks on aghast. One picks an old coat off the clothes rack, and one says, "Look, it is only an old coat." The child breaks into fitful giggles. Has one *named* the object which struck terror in the child? On the contrary, one has totally *misnamed* it, as regards its nature in the child's precious orientation. To have *named* it would have been to call out, "Away, thou hideous monster—thou cackling demon of hell, away!" and henceforth that corner would be the very altar of terror. One casts out demons by a vocabulary of *conversion*, by an *incongruous* naming, by calling them *the very thing in all the world they are not:* old coats.

The notion of exorcism by misnomer ("organized bad taste") may also explain away various other apparent conflicts among psychoanalytic treatments. Thus, Adler frames his cure from an entirely different point of view, stressing not the *amative* interests of Freud but the *combative* interests. He says that the patient is suffering from an attempt to compensate for early impressions of inferiority. Here too is a concept highly valuable in disclosing the rationality of conduct which had been labeled irrational. In the first place, just as it is quite obvious that everyone must love or hate something, so it seems inevitable that one should have been inferior to something, if only a mountain or a continent.

Much of Adler's technique is devoted to bringing out the antagonistic aspects of the patient's concerns until the patient is extremely resentful; then Adler undermines this resentment by a deliberately incongruous response, accepting the resentment as the *normal* and *expected* thing. This procedure, suggestive in itself as a method of conversion downwards, by making it clear that the patient's focal interests are really nothing to be so excited about, is also backed by the introduction of an alien vocabulary which is "unsuited" to the altar of the patient's distress.[1]

The conflict of exorcism by misnomer also has some bearing upon the insanity of such writers as Nietzsche and Swift, who were both preoccupied with the problems of conversion. These men devoted their energies to a *conversion upwards,* a one-way process of magnification, a *writing large* that lacked a compensatory process of *writing down.* Nietzsche keyed his concerns to the magnitude of the tragic, his typically schizophrenic dislike of normal laughter refusing to permit him any humor but the grotesque, sardonic kind. As a consequence, he lived enwrapped in loneliness, thinking in terms of grandeur, of vast historic sweeps, of long vistas as seen from the tops of cold and sterile mountains, a forbidding imagery which comes tragically to its perfection in his *Zarathustra,* a book which he adulated with all the reverence that a deeply pious nature could possibly bring to the honor of a Cathedral erected above his own profoundest misery. Yet he seems himself to have felt the need of a complementary process, since he tries repeatedly to put his poignant work forward as a "Happy Science." An aspect of this same feeling is to be seen in that eerie cult of exaltation which we find in the *Rausch* scenes of *Zarathustra,* the imaginary alchoholic indulgences and frater-

---

[1] The weakness in the various individualistic schemes of cure offered since the breakdown of the religious rationalization seems to arise from the fact that the resultant socialization is but partial. The texture of new meanings is not rich enough, and does not enjoy sufficient reenforcement from society as a whole, to make it soundly communicative. It is *compensatory* rather than *integral.*

nizations of a man who testified that the slightest touch of liquor could set his mind into a painful whirl for many hours.

As for Swift: he too showed that he restlessly sought a technique of *conversion downwards,* some mitigating device which would enable him to call the monsters of his imagination old coats. As evidence that he felt this need, do we not have his simple reversal of relationship, from that of Gulliver big, Lilliputians little, to that of Gulliver little, Brobdingnagians big? But the true nature of his ways is revealed in the "synthesis": Yahoos crude, Houyhnhnms refined. To look at all three relationships is to realize that, whatever their reversals of proportion in the literal sense, they were all *au fond* the same: the *magnification* of human despicability, the emphasizing of greed, ignorance, coarseness, treachery, and the like, in sustained imagery. As a consequence, Swift lived among monsters—and to live among monsters is to live on the edge of hell.

Swift was, as Coleridge says of him with pointedness quite to our purpose, *"Anima Rabelaisii habitans in sicco*—the soul of Rabelais dwelling in a dry place." For it is precisely the ways of Rabelais that might best illustrate the fullness of a two-way process, the hearty shuttling back and forth between conversion upwards and conversion downwards, as he now approached the "spiritualities" of the Church through the terminology of gluttony and license, and then again "projected" the most riotous human appetites upward into their own noble, speculative and imaginative transmogrifications, giving us not only the swinishness that underlay the structure of virtue, but also the wide reaches of understanding that grew out of this very swinishness.

Conversion and the Lex Continui

Conversions are generally managed by the search for a "graded series" whereby we move step by step from some kind of event, in which the presence of a certain factor is sanctioned in the language of common sense, to other events in which this factor had not previously been noted. The thinker attempts to establish a continuity for arriving at conclusions which might seem abrupt and paradoxical if the two ends of his series were juxtaposed abruptly, without the interpolation of a gradient. Thus, in harmonic theory, the composer Arnold Schoenberg takes us step by step from the methods of classical music to the methods which he employs —and if we follow his gradients we are imperceptibly eased from a region of sound where the logic of composition is generally apparent into a region of sound which might have seemed to the uninstructed hearer as chaotic. The ideal gradients are found in the recordings of the physicist, as when he shows us by thermometer readings the quantitative critical points at which water is converted into substances so qualitatively different as ice and steam. In the psychological realm, the search for gradients is more complex and dubious—but the clear assumption of the *lex continui* is to be seen in both animal and abnormal psychology, where the thinker notes the workings of anguish or training as revealed in clinic or laboratory, and seeks to infer the presence of the same basic processes in normal human life. We have attempted to obey the *lex continui* in our treatment of piety by a series of steps moving from religion (where the presence of piety is linguistically acknowledged) to the habits of the gashouse gang (a kind of conduct from which common usage had excluded pious ingredients).

The significant shortcoming of this method as a way of understanding human nature lies in the fact that it omits the critical points. It may show the presence of the same factor in normal human life that we discern in animal or abnormal psychology; but it cannot state, with the precision of the thermometer, the exact stage at which the *qualities* of the experience change. It is better adapted for showing that water, steam, and ice are all H_2O than for discovering the important readings of temperature at which H_2O undergoes

such significant transformations. And human experience being essentially qualitative, this failure to name the critical
points is admittedly a grave fault. In mental happenings, a
quantitative increase in complexity may cause a complete
qualitative transformation as distinct as the difference between water and ice. And the *rationale* of pre-evolutionary
thought, which refuses to consider things in the light of their
genesis, is founded on the feeling that, unless you can name
the critical points at which qualitative transformations take
place, your account of derivations is too truncated to be of
real service. This would be the basis of a theologian's refusal,
for instance, to accept Marxian or psychoanalytic explanations
of the genesis of religion.

But let us make up a sample set of gradients (having in
mind our technique of conversion) to illustrate the full scope
of the choices which the principle of the *lex continui* can place
before us. In his *Nature and Life*, Whitehead has written:
"Philosophy is the product of wonder." It so happens that
Veblen situated the origin of philosophic, or scientific speculation in "idle curiosity." Now, if you key up *idle curiosity,*
you might get *curiosity* pure and simple. If you key up *curiosity,* you get *interest.* Key up *interest,* and you get *wonder.*
Key up *wonder,* you get *reverence.* And so to *awe, fear,* and
dread. Thus, by conversion upwards, we can modulate from
Veblen's formula, through Whitehead's, to an assertion that
"Philosophy is the product of terror."

The gloomier colors of our spectrum would suggest an element of hypochondriasis in scientific speculation, and might
explain why one of our earlier stargazers was actually awe-
struck as he turned from his telescope and announced, "I have
found a hole in the heavens!" It so happens that he had not;
the heavens were still intact; he had merely found a dark
nebula that blotted out the stars behind it—but this feature
need not detain us here. It is his awe, verging upon fright,
that is relevant to our sample set of gradients. Furthermore,
Rivers has noted the fact that patients may reconcile themselves to their disease by becoming engrossed in its symptoms.

He calls such adjustment hypochondriasis. We may clearly discern its presence in the speculations of *Hamlet*, Job, Ecclesiastes, Jeremiah, and Eliot's *The Waste Land*. Might we not also note it among scientists who announce that they are "merely diagnosing our social difficulties, merely facing the facts, without regard for a remedy"?

Further extensions are imaginable. For instance, we could convert downwards, going from *idle curiosity* to *play*, thereby getting to a choice which particularly distinguished many theories of the nineteenth century following Schiller. Or we might project *fear* at a tangent, getting by continuity to such exegetic possibilities as *defense*, since fear suggests the need of self-protection. *Defense* (or *combat*) in turn could be split into the dichotomous concepts, *courage* or *cowardice*. Our choice along the path of gradients now runs:

Philosophy is the product of play
                idle curiosity
                curiosity
                interest
                wonder
                reverence
                awe
                fear ⎫ defense (combat)
                dread ⎬
                terror ⎭ cowardice; courage.

Note that the establishment of the series itself does not automatically provide a clue as to which point we should select as the *essence* of the entire scale. One's choice usually flows from other aspects of his orientation, or from the particular purpose which his series is designed to fulfill. We have already noted the therapeutic reasons that influence choice, in the curative device of conversion downwards. But we should also note that a certain degree of conversion upwards may be curative on occasion. *Wonder*, for instance, is much more in keeping with the usual standards of decency than *play*, unless one hastens to broaden the concept of play until play itself has been converted upwards, magnified beyond its ordinary connotations. And a man whose general scheme of values would lead him to balk at the choice of *fear* or *cowardice*, might find no trouble in selecting *defense* or *courage*. That doughty warrior Nietzsche might have preferred another aspect of defense, *combat*—and Piaget's researches into the development of logic from *quarreling* would seem to provide some justification for this choice.

Another interesting attempt to find the source of complex mental structures is suggested in the literature of mysticism, where there so often recurs the compelling image of the *abyss*, some aweful internal chasm (Eliot: "we are the hollow men"), a sense of distance, division, or vertigo which has at times been verbalized by reference to a "geographical" place, the bottomless pit of hell. This image may arise from some neural dissociation which, involving the two lobes of the brain, is sensed by the "shut in" type of mind but not interpreted with complete accuracy. In any event, we note the presence of the image strongly in Milton's epic, with its startling pictures of interstellar space—and it was Milton who distinguished between his poetic glorifications and his prose vituperation by the metaphor of the *right* and *left* hand.

Our contemporary mystic poet, Hart Crane, seems to have revealed a similar sense of the abyss in his choice of the *bridge* as his key symbol. Socially, the division was observable in his unhappy conflict between homosexual and heterosexual leanings. And it may be more than a coincidence that this symbolist ended his life symbolically, by plunging into the great abyss of mid-ocean. In any event, it is conceivable that a purely subjective sense of the abyss could be converted downwards by actually going into high places and gazing from them, thus bringing the experience within the negotiable realm of factual objects. The curative effect of such a process might account for the almost mystical exaltation we have noted in the descriptions of mountain-climbing—and conversely, it might justify us in looking for an "abyss-motif" behind the cult of flight.

From *Permanence and Change: An Anatomy of Purpose* (2nd ed.; Los Altos, Calif.: Hermes Publications, 1954), pp. 125-136, 142-147.

Stances

(1937)

Acceptance and Passivity

Could we not say that all symbolic structures are designed to produce such "acceptance" in one form or another? In its most trivial form (where a good device is made sentimental by oversimplification) we get the Pollyanna solution: If you break your leg, thank God you didn't break your neck. We see it in the attitude behind the vulgar assurance that it always rains when you forget your umbrella. We have it when the fox, unable to reach the grapes, decided they were sour. We find it in the jokes whereby men, in the face of danger, dwarf the danger ("trench humor" that maintains "trench morale"). It is said of Democritus, that when he imagined a universe made of tiny atoms bumping and combining with one another, he *laughed*. Why did Democritus laugh? Perhaps he laughed because, by his materialist doctrine, he had "debunked" the gods. He "accepted" the world by ruling out the threats of ghostly vengeance. He was in the trenches of metaphysics, and materialism was the humor for his trench morale.

"Frames of acceptance" are not the same as *passiveness*. Since they name both friendly and unfriendly forces, they fix attitudes that prepare for combat. They draw the lines of battle—and they appear "passive" only to one whose frame would persuade him to draw the line of battle differently. Aquinas was as realistic as Marx, for instance, in recognizing the existence of social classes. It was the bourgeois interregnum that tried to eliminate them by fiat, in treating the bourgeois class as universal mankind. The difference between Marx and Aquinas is in the attitude (incipient program of action) taken towards the existence of classes. Since Aquinas, following Augustine, looked upon classes (with attendant phenomena of government, property, and slavery) as punishment for the fall of man, his frame was designed to accept the inevitability of classes, and to build a frame of action accordingly. Marx, on the other hand, accepted the *need of eliminating classes,* hence drew the line of battle differently.

It was the bourgeois attitude that came nearest to passivity in this respect, because of an understressing that was often purely sentimental. In its heyday, following comparative victory over the nobility, the bourgeois frame simply smeared the issue out of mind. It "rejected" class morality by "accepting" the doctrine that the resources of private initiative were equally available to all. And many centuries elapsed before people's characters were molded in accordance with this frame.[1]

All three frames would be active with relation to the line between "friendly" and "unfriendly" that each drew in its own way. Those who call it "passive" usually mean that they would draw the critical line of action elsewhere.

Rejection

"Rejection" is but a by-product of "acceptance." It involves primarily a matter of emphasis. It takes its color from an attitude towards some reigning symbol of authority, stressing a *shift in the allegiance* to symbols of authority. It is the heretical aspect of an orthodoxy—and as such, it has much in

[1] The maximum development from a subsistence economy to a money economy was not attained until the period just preceding the rise of Fascism with its great hordes of state laborers that show a marked analogy to the feudal ideal. The peak was probably reached when the genius of capitalism had become sufficiently implemented by the money market and the private control of credit (the symbolic medium of exchange) to force the "money crop" idea upon the agrarians, the group that clung most tenaciously to the vestiges of a purely subsistence economy, and hence were the last to adopt a *purely financial* concept of efficiency in living and producing.

common with the "frame of acceptance" that it rejects. It somewhat robs a thinker of his birthright, his right to "consume" reality without regurgitation. If the king is well thought of in many quarters, the man who would build his frame to accept the necessity of *deposing* the king is almost necessarily, by the tactics of the case, shunted into a negativistic emphasis. Such rigors may explain the fact that the Communist Manifesto begins with a terroristic metaphor. At this strategic point (for beginnings and endings are particularly strategic, the first setting the tone for the reception of one's message, the second clinching the thesis before a final parting) the authors were presumably led by the power of the orthodox authority to depict their project for redemption, in negativistic terms, as a *specter that haunts;* and in parting they address themselves to the *anger of slaves.* This polemic, negativistic genius (stressing the *no* more than the *yes*) throws the emphasis stylistically upon the partiality of rejection rather than the completeness of acceptance.

The relation that frames of acceptance bear to symbols of authority inevitably puts the symbolist of change at this tactical disadvantage, warping somewhat the perfect roundness of his utterance. There is no "no" in music—and educators of children have also suggested the possibility that there is no "no" in the psychology of attention. The full strategy for saying *"don't* do that" is *"do* do this." The issue may throw light upon the resistances of our countrymen, who were long trained in the Emerson-Whitman-James mode of emphasis, and constructed their notions of sociality upon it.

The preference is grounded in Christian apologetics. Thus, when the increasing economic strain of late feudalism was making men restless and bellicose, when their growing "mobility," under the stimulus of economic frustration, manifested itself first in pilgrimage and eventually took the form of militant crusades, the Church quickly put forward beneficent fictions of penance and indulgence whereby the mounting pugnacity could be "saved" as far as possible. The blood that was let was let for God and personal salvation. The churchmen were saying, in effect: "Where there is unseemly work to be done, let us at least do it in a seemly vocabulary."

As a given historical frame nears the point of cracking, strained by the rise of new factors it had not originally taken into account, its adherents employ its genius casuistically to extend it as far as possible. Thus the Churchmen invented peaceful fictions for war, in their simplicity probably hoping that, if and when the wars abated, the genius inherent in the pacific terms could again express itself in less imperfect modes. (This casuistic stretching, incidentally, is to be noted also in the judicial interpretations by which the American Constitution has been expanded to permit a freedom for corporations not foreseen at the time of its adoption. The stretchers pre-empt the "acceptance" emphasis, thus forcing the "rejection" emphasis upon the opposition.)

We find the "rejection" feature arising with Machiavelli, who crystallized the shift to civil coordinates of authority, and whose *"Realpolitik"* laid the foundations for the materialistic emphasis, in putting forward the *cult of power* as the basis of human motivation. It is present in Hobbes, with the picturesque *homo homini lupus* and *bellum omnium contra omnes* formulae as the groundwork of his monarchic system. In the realm of paradox, it gains ground in Mandeville's "Fable of the Bees," whose clever subtitle, "Private vices public virtues," is well on the road to the commercialist "transvaluation of values." The new economic structure has, by this time, revealed its outlines with sufficient clarity to necessitate a new code of morals—and Mandeville's fable radically reverses the Church's attitude towards a key value, personal ambition. In the Church's moral scheme, ambition had been a major vice. Mandeville playfully speculated upon the possibility of enshrining it as the major virtue. He fabulously suggested that if people were greedy and pushing enough in personal enterprise, they would produce an abundance of commodities whereby the whole community would profit.

In the spirit of high comedy, Mandeville dealt with the same shift in values that Shakespeare had considered tragically in *Macbeth*. Macbeth is the poetic adumbration of the "Faustian man," who would fulfill his destiny at all costs. He stands at the turning point between the feudal attitude towards ambition, as *punishable pride*, and the commercial attitude towards ambition, as the *essence of vocation*. Shakespeare heralds the new, while fearing it in terms of the old. In Mandeville the conflict is considered less drastically, though he still draws upon it for his literary effects.[2]

By the time we get to Adam Smith, the new code has gained sufficient authority to be framed as *orthodoxy*. Smith proceeds simply by rationalizing Mandeville *without* the paradox; ambition becomes a private virtue because it is a public virtue. The utilitarians completed his theory. Thus, in England the "transvaluation of values" had gained codification and authoritative backing long before Nietzsche, in more feudalistic Germany, began to put it forward challengingly and confusedly. And Marx, whose English training had shown him its ascendancy, laid out the frame for its *rejection*. Ironically, he came before Spencer, whose *optimistic* picture of disintegration (epitomized in his definition of "progress" as a development from homogeneity to heterogeneity) completed the intellectual architecture of Adam Smith's economics.

The Changing Emphasis of Frames

When surveying the historic curve on the graph of Western culture, we can better understand what was accomplished by the shift from the classical emphasis upon resignation to the liberal ("Faustian") emphasis upon freedom. The revolu-

---

[2] Though this lineage makes no attempt to be complete, perhaps we should also include Marlowe's Dr. Faustus, where the new values (of "power-knowledge") are introduced with fearsome connotations. The drama itself shows closer connections in form with the church "morality play" out of which secular tragedy developed. Marlowe's ambiguity, in confronting the new bourgeois standards from the old feudal point of view, is even greater than Shakespeare's, as was his personal irritability.

tionary philosophy of business enterprise served to democratize a sense of personal mastery hitherto reserved to but a few— and even they, with their stress upon pre-established *status*, had not generally thought of their privileges in terms of *advancement*. Machiavelli provided the turbulent Renaissance "prince" with the beginnings of "success" coordinates. The later, more exclusively commercial focus, seems to have been sharpened by the textbooks on accountancy that began gaining attention shortly after him. Particularly, as Sombart has observed, the perfection of double-entry bookkeeping, with its clear visualization of profit and loss in monetary terms, prepared the way for the abstract concepts of "production for gain" that rationalized investment and efficiency in accordance with purely capitalist criteria. Here began the attempt to shift from the "prosperity of poverty" to the "economy of plenty."

The earlier tests of human effort had been *qualitative*— and when you organize a mode of operation about qualities (standards of "good living," mainly grounded in the authority of custom), your policies cannot readily meet the requirements of discursive reason. You become entangled in blunt assertions of the *de gustibus non disputandum est* variety. Accountancy offered a *quantitative* device for making action rational. The merchant did not have to juggle tenuous notions of vice and virtue when judging his plan of action. He simply consulted his ledgers, and the plan proved "good" if his balance at the end of the year showed income outweighing costs. The "rational" henceforth ceased to be the mere "handmaiden of faith"—it became the very essence of method. There is no point in either saluting or regretting the shift. Here we need but observe it.

And we may further speculate upon the great *relief* that the liberal doctrine must have brought to men, made restless by the Church's organized attempts to legislate against the genius of the glandular system, and by the extent to which the privileged had "moved in on" the people's attitude of obedience until acceptance of the *status quo* had become almost physically impossible. The psychological equivalent of the attempt to "resign" oneself under such conditions was neurosis. The religious rationalization could provide a vent for an incredible amount of neurotic agitation—but in time these resources also were strained to their breaking point.

At such a critical juncture, the commercial, quantitative tests for rationalizing conduct were a very happy invention. They opened up a new field of effort, further widened by the discovery of America and the development of technology. For several centuries, they made a population of Fausts *possible,* by providing the historical environment in which such a "culture" (in the bacteriological sense) could grow and multiply. The range of *opportunity* for individualistic assertion was widened, permitting a percentage of individualism that, in any other setting, would probably have led to chaos.

Instead of leading to chaos, the new material and moral resources were eventually able to adapt the notions of "profit" so completely to the secular frame that the zeal of the religious wars abated. There resulted several centuries of fairly rational *organization.* But now, after nearly half a millennium, these new resources seem to have been exploited to the point where they in turn are nearing their "Malthusian limits." The liberal habits of private enterprise "proliferated," like yeast in the mash, until they could not proliferate much further. The by-product of their activity (the "alcohol" they generated) now threatens their extinction (a metaphorical way of rephrasing the thesis that liberalism, like *any* cultural trend long followed, must produce its "inner contradictions").

Any organized mode of understanding and acting offers its own possibilities of laxity. In time, there occurs a pro-liferation of the habits that take advantage of these oppor-tunities. The exploitation of such habits will itself become organized, "bureaucratized," until the given mode of un-derstanding and acting has been stretched to its "Malthusian limits." A culture then faces a crisis, the need for a "revolution" of sufficient scope to make new opportunities for exploitation possible. Insofar as the new opportunities are not provided, we get decadence, neurosis, anger (expressing itself in either external war or internal antagonisms, the devices whereby a people "projects" its uneasiness upon a scapegoat).

Many have charted the difficulties of such a critical period, as they apply to "frames of acceptance." The ideal conditions for thought arise when the world is deemed about as satisfactory as we can make it, and thinkers of all sorts collaborate in constructing a vast collective mythology whereby people can be at home in that world. Conflicts are bridged symbolically; one tries to mitigate conflict by the mediating devices of poetry and religion, rather than to accentuate the harshness. Such is man's "natural" vocation. It makes for the well-rounded philosophy of an Aristotle, who contributed much to the Summa of Aquinas. It seeks to develop attitudes of resignation whereby we may make the best of things as they are.

But the inexorable workings of the "neo-Malthusian" principle eventually make such frames drastically inadequate. New material arises, if only as "by-products" of the cultural pattern. Marx has shown the effects of new productive techniques in this respect. While the frame centers the attention upon some relationships, by this very thoroughness it obscures the perception of new factors that are of critical importance. Or it may induce thinkers to damn the new factors as *symptoms,* without disclosing the causes of the symptoms. We note this tendency towards sermon and invective particularly in the thinking of the Church, where men trained in prayer are particularly prone (under the promptings of their "occupational psychosis") to handle all untoward issues verbally, by benediction or anathema: they would "legislate" a disorder out of existence. But the tendency is not unknown even to secular thinkers. Note, for instance, the proliferation of laws under parliamentary governments, where the ready availability of law-making has invited people to "move in on" this convenience to such an extent that legislation often becomes hardly more than a kind of public prayer.

Frames stressing the ingredient of *rejection* tend to lack the well-rounded quality of a *complete* here-and-now philosophy. They make for fanaticism, the singling-out of one factor above others in the charting of human relationships. Their simplest caricature is the "money crank," who would shape all life's purposes around some project for tinkering with the *symbols* of exchange without concern for the underlying economic factors and psychological attributes that go with them. Marx, being born into the great century of rejection philosophies, discloses the scars of his environment; nevertheless he did unquestionably lay the foundations for a vast public enterprise out of which a new frame of acceptance could be constructed. Arising among idealists, he caught the genius of realism. His project, we might say, was pre-realism or pro-realism, a here-and-now philosophy designed mainly for action during the late-capitalist interregnum, but containing some ingredients for a post-capitalist reintegration.

The romanticism that is contemporaneous with Marx, and left its imprint upon his writings (particularly in his stressing of antithesis) is cluttered with rejection frames having varying degrees of accuracy and thoroughness. Goethe had both welcomed and feared his Faust, the man of driving personal ambition who would assert his genius even at the risk of partnership with the devil. This "tragic ambiguity," whereby a growing trend is at once recommended and punished, is present also in Shakespeare's treatment of Macbeth, who represents the new bourgeois concepts of ambition in grotesque guise. In confronting the emergent capitalist standards, Shakespeare retained many conservative, feudal norms of value. The result, made by the incongruous juxtaposition of both conservative and revolutionary frames, was a "tragic ambiguity" whereby he gave expression to the rising trends, but gave them the forbidding connotations of criminality.

Byron, admired by Goethe, gave us "Faustian" heroes who were the lineal descendants of Milton's Satan (the creation of a man whose political allegiances made him a symbolic regicide). As a whole, those who had religious leanings, but were sufficiently affected by science to become skeptical of the Church's dogmas, tended to "reject" the world symbolically by entering the monastery of art. Wagner's "temple of art" stretches before him and after him. A kind of "two-world" scheme arose, the antithetical worlds of the practical and the esthetic, with a few writers like Mann trying, by mixture of irony and melancholy, to mediate between them. Such frames can be labeled, as you prefer, either by their "acceptance" of the esthetic or their "rejection" of the practical.

From *Attitudes Toward History* (2nd ed.; Los Altos, Calif.: Hermes Publications, 1959), pp. 19-30.

From

Poetic Categories

(*1937*)

Introduction

Our way of approaching the structures of symbolism might be profitably tested by the examination of various literary categories, as each of the great poetic forms stresses its own peculiar way of building the mental equipment (meanings, attitudes, character) by which one handles the significant factors of his time.

We shall begin with the epic, as a typical frame of symbolic adjustment under primitive conditions. We do get sophisticated imitations of the epic, such as the *Aeneid,* in highly "enlightened" eras. But the form arises under primitive, noncommercial, conditions. Writers have remarked on the *deliberately* archaic quality of the Homeric poems, which may suggest a certain nostalgia behind their composition, as though the new ways had already begun to make themselves felt while the materials of primitive living were still largely present, there being just enough of the new to make appreciation of the old more poignant.

In the case of Virgil, the prestige of Homer might be enough to account for his choice of form. Also, he wrote to celebrate the rise of Augustus, who marked the turn away from the *laissez-faire* period in Roman enterprise, and founded the bureaucratic modes of governmental administration, under central imperial authority, that would eventually lead to the crystallization of the Roman state. From the time of Augustus, "prosperity" in the business sense of the term was on the wane. Roman efficiency, backed by bureaucratic organization, and possessing such valuable granaries as Egypt, could garner much material wealth; and agricultural science, perfected during Hellenism, could increase and regularize productivity; but the heyday of private investment, that had "flowered" just before the rise of Caesar, was over. Under the emperors, the speculations of the *equites,* who had mulcted the Roman provinces, were radically curbed. Public enterprises again came to the fore. Even at the time of imperial decay, when one soldier after another seized power at Rome, advancement for the great bulk of the army was as regular as among the underlings of a modern insurance company. Soldiering eventually became a trade, and on the whole a very stable one, without great risks. The empire built an invisible Chinese wall about its borders, and perfected an internal network of communications that long made it able to resist the sporadic, unorganized pressure at the frontiers. Business slowly abated to a standstill—the *novus homo* of Cicero's day no longer (as Belloc would say) gave the "tone" to the state—the fixation of class status became the rule.

This trend began with the reforms of Augustus, and Virgil was his poet. As such, he may have been sensitive to the course of events in their incipient form, a frequent characteristic of great poets. By this interpretation, it would be not merely the prestige of Homer that prompted Virgil to select the epic form. It would also be the fact that the epic is indigenous with the period *preceding* commercial enlightenment, and Virgil's position is somewhat analogous since he was writing to celebrate the *close* of commercial freedom.

The epic is designed, then, under primitive conditions, to make men "at home in" those conditions. It "accepts" the rigors of war (the basis of the tribe's success) by magnifying the role of warlike hero. Such magnification serves two purposes: It lends dignity to the necessities of existence, "advertising" courage and individual sacrifice for group advantage—and it enables the humble man to share the worth of the hero by the process of "identification." The hero, real or legendary, thus risks himself and dies that others may be *vicariously* heroic (a variant of the symbolic cluster in Christianity whereby the victim of original sin could share vicariously in the perfection of Christ by his membership in the Church, the *corpus Christi*). The social value of such a pattern resides in its ability to make humility and self-glorification *work together:* the sense of one's limitations (in comparison with the mighty figure of the legend) provides one with a realistic attitude for gauging his personal resources, while his vicarious kinship with the figure gives him the distinction necessary for the needs of self-justification.[1]

The thought suggests what psychological devastation would follow from a complete adherence to the "debunking" school of biography whereby, in destroying the dignity of great legendary or historical characters, we automatically destroy ourselves. The heroic legend is saying, in effect, as Goethe said to Schopenhauer: "We can only get from life what we put into it"; and if we are greedy, we had better put in a great deal. Since the epic heroes mediate between men and gods, having the qualities of both, their divinity is generally "humanized" (being given, as James would say, "cash value") by the presence of a flaw, as the one vulnerable spot on Siegfried or Achilles, or Christ's predestination for the cross.

[1] Insofar as the tragically and epically heroic approaches a purely non-religious emphasis, it approaches the risks of coxcombry. The proper ingredient of humility is retained only when one's identification with the godlike hero is discounted by the realization that one is *not* the hero. A religious concept of the hero's *divinity* induces this discounting. But insofar as the hero becomes purely secular, it is easier for the non-hero to make his identification with the hero *complete*.

The process of identification thus becomes more accessible, and incidentally dignifies any sense of persecution that may possess the individual, who may also feel himself marked for disaster. This sense of a flaw serves happily to promote an openness to realistic admonition—the invitation to seek the flaw in oneself promotes in the end the attitude of *resignation* (which, when backed by a *well-rounded* symbolic structure, is nothing other than the inventory of one's *personal* limits).

Tragedy

The resignation of tragedy is based upon this same sense of personal limits; but the cultural materials with which the tragic playwright works are much more urban, complex, sophisticated than those that prevailed at the rise of the primitive epic. Though the same magical patterns of fatality, magnification, and humility are present, they are submerged beneath a more "enlightened" scheme of causal relationships. Greek tragedy flowered when the individualistic development of commerce had been strongly superimposed upon the earlier primitive-collectivist structure. The fear of self-aggrandizement was strong, as is shown in the fact that commercial enterprise was mainly entrusted to the "metics," foreigners who were imported to manage the interchange of goods for profit.

The period of human relationships *preceding* the rise of trade is close to the psychology of the "potlach," where goods are distributed by promiscuous *giving* rather than by *getting;* the shift from one attitude to the other is a basic "transvaluation of values." In the Greek cities, the shift of attitude is revealed in the changing uses to which the institution of the "guest-friend" was put, as commerce gradually expanded to confuse the bearings of the earlier culture. The visiting trader enjoyed rights of protection only by coming as a "friend" of a local citizen. Eventually, with the spread of trade, the fiction was expanded casuistically until we find some prominent citizen acting as "guest-friend" for a whole city (the original magic of an intimate guest-relationship thus being obliterated by an enlightened extension into "quantity production" of impersonal guest-friendships).[2]

However, the greater complexity of relationships that went with the development of trade and urban living led to a proliferation of the *forensic*, as exemplified in the law courts and in parliamentary procedure. Out of legal sophistication there grew the vast *metaphysical* structures, that eventually imposed *scientific* concepts of causality upon the earlier patterns of magic and religion. The new attitude reached its culmination *explicitly* in Aristotle, but we find it *implicitly* in the great writers of tragedy that preceded him. Their plays, we might say, are complex trials by jury, with plaintiff, defendant, attorneys, judges, and jury all rolled into one—or, otherwise stated, we get in one piece the offense, the sentence, and the expiation. The magical concepts of fatality remain (the *participation mystique* whereby divine dispositions are concerned with human destinies), but they must be fused with the new forensic materials. Hence, the events of a tragedy are made to grow out of one another in keeping with the logic of scientific cogency, the Q.E.D. of Euclid and the political oration.

The rise of business individualism sharpened the awareness of personal ambition as a motive in human acts, but the great tragic playwrights were pious, orthodox, conservative, "reactionary" in their attitude towards it; hence they made pride, *hubris*, the basic sin, and "welcomed" it by tragic ambiguity, surrounding it with the connotations of crime.[3]

---

[2] We may note a similar trend in the Egyptian "democratization" of Osirianism, whereby the sale of priestly incantations, first confined to the immortalizing of the Pharaoh, gradually spread to all the people, with a corresponding drop in quality, or in Europe when, as Strachey observes in his *Coming Struggle for Power*, the sale of indulgences was finally organized on a business basis. "Demoralization" always occurs when commercial rationalism seeks to retain the co-ordinates of magic or religion out of which it developed.

[3] This statement of the case might be a partial answer to those who ask whether a given writer of tragedy is "progressive" or "reactionary." Tragedy deals in crime—and any incipient trend will first be felt as

Their frame of acceptance admonished one to "resign" himself to a sense of his limitations. They *feared* good fortune, as the first sign of punishment from the gods. Among contemporary psychologists, schooled to the norms of bourgeois thought, this attitude is usually considered as an aspect of pathology.

Comedy, Humor, the Ode

Comedy, Meredith has said, is the most civilized form of art. What reason is there to question him? The class that can produce good comedy is about as happy as can be. True, the adjustment, though admirable in itself, is often shown by subsequent events to have been a very dangerous one, as though a contented village were to have evolved its culture at the edge of a sleeping volcano that is already, in its "subconscious" depths, preparing to break forth and scatter destruction.

We should account for this dramatic irony, that subsequent history adds to our interpretation of the happy time, by suggesting that the materials incorporated within the frame are never broad enough to encompass all the necessary attitudes. Not all the significant cultural factors are given the importance

---

crime, by reason of its conflict with established values. But tragedy deals *sympathetically* with crime. Even though the criminal is finally sentenced to be punished, we are made to feel that his offense is our offense, and at the same time the offense is dignified by nobility of style.

Caroline Spurgeon notes the great part that the imagery of *ill-fitting clothes* plays in giving the tone of *Macbeth*. And ill-fitting clothes are *grotesque;* they *caricature* a man. Shakespeare's stressing of a grotesque ingredient in the offender might suggest that in this case the weight of the stylistic admonitions *against* the crime is stronger than in most cases of tragic sympathy with crime. The ambiguous endorsement by dignification is much weaker than, let us say, the treatment of Brutus and Cassius, offenders against "ambitious" Caesar. Again: Macbeth's thoughts are *witches*—these subhuman creatures are the dramatic objectification of his subjective state (a modern Expressionist dramatist might have shown them coming out of his head, as Strindberg made his characters walk through walls). Like the ill-fitting clothes, they caricature his destiny.

that a total vision of reality would require. Class interests provide the cues that distort the interpretative frame, making its *apparent* totality function as an *actual* partiality. From the organization of class interests there inevitably follow over-emphases and underemphases: favorable factors are seen too favorably, unfavorable factors are neglected. While the thinker trains himself and his audience to balance on one tightrope, history is stretching a tightrope elsewhere. Hence, as regards *all* the necessities, the very glories of the frame become its menace.

"Class morality" functions as "cultural lag," insofar as another class of people arises whose situation is not accurately located by the attitudinizings of the frame. And insofar as those for whom the frame is comparatively adequate are kept by their own material emphases from noting its limitations, it is the "culturally dispossessed" whom they accuse of "attitu-dinizing" (the new attitudes, not being their attitudes, are felt as attitudes, rather than as "truth"). So, for instance, Samuel Johnson's aptnesss at purveying comic humanism of the sort desired by his employers, led him to misgauge the significance of the incoming romanticism. And Pope, for all his incipiently romantic insistence that great art overrides established rules, tended to excoriate the new emphasis as bad taste (*whose* bad taste?), without concern for the necessities that stimulated writers to outrage the established canons of taste. A frame becomes deceptive when it provides too great plausibility for the writer who would *condemn symptoms* without being able to gauge the *causal pressure* behind the symptoms.

Like tragedy, comedy warns against the dangers of pride, but its emphasis shifts from *crime* to *stupidity*. Shakespeare, whose tragedies gravitate towards melodrama (notably in a work like *Othello*) required *villains* to make his plot work. Henry James made an essentially comic observation when saying that his plots required the intervention of *fools*. Antony, in becoming the active agent of the plot after the murder of Caesar, suggests a third instrument: the "good" character activated by motives of justifiable vengeance.

The progress of humane enlightenment can go no further than in picturing people not as *vicious,* but as *mistaken.* When you add that people are *necessarily* mistaken, that *all* people are exposed to situations in which they must act as fools, that *every* insight contains its own special kind of blindness, you complete the comic circle, returning again to the lesson of humility that underlies great tragedy. The audience, from its vantage point, sees the operation of errors that the characters of the play cannot see; thus seeing from two angles at once, it is chastened by dramatic irony; it is admonished to remember that when intelligence means *wisdom* (in contrast with the modern tendency to look upon intelligence as merely a *coefficient of power* for heightening our ability to get things, be they good or bad), it requires fear, resignation, the sense of limits, as an important ingredient.

Comedy requires the maximum of forensic complexity. In the tragic plot the *deus ex machina* is always lurking, to give events a fatalistic turn in accordance with the old *"participation"* pattern whereby men anthropomorphize nature, feeling its force as the taking of sides with them or against them. Comedy must develop logical forensic causality to its highest point, calling not upon astronomical marvels to help shape the plot, but completing the process of internal organization whereby each event is deduced "syllogistically" from the premises of the informing situation. Comedy deals with *man in society,* tragedy with the *cosmic man.* (This emphasis, after the organized documentation that followed Darwin, eventually led to Hardy's kind of tragedy, *man in nature.* In classic tragedy the motivating forces are superhuman, in romantic-naturalist tragedy they are *inhuman.*) Comedy is essentially *humane,* leading in periods of comparative stability to the comedy of manners, the dramatization of quirks and foibles. But it is not necessarily confined to drama. The best of Bentham, Marx, and Veblen is high comedy.

In contemporary drama we find it revealed effetely in a play like Coward's *Bitter Sweet,* where the very title suggests a rudimentary kind of comic ambivalence: we must take the bitter with the sweet. The playwright exemplifies this lesson none too maturely in a plot where the heroine, unable to choose between two lovers, ends by taking both. Undecided whether to order sherbet or cake, she "resigns herself" to the necessity of ordering sherbet *and* cake. The "curative value" of such a happy thought seems to have been appreciated by the public, ever in search of artistic inventions whereby redemption comes easy.

We might, however, note an important distinction between comedy and humor, that is disclosed when we approach art forms as "frames of acceptance," as "strategies" for living. Humor is the opposite of the heroic. The heroic promotes acceptance by *magnification*, making the hero's character as great as the situation he confronts, and fortifying the nonheroic individual vicariously, by identification with the hero; but humor reverses the process: it takes up the slack between the momentousness of the situation and the feebleness of those in the situation by *dwarfing the situation*. It converts downwards, as the heroic converts upwards. Hence it does not make for so completely well-rounded a frame of acceptance as comedy, since it tends to gauge the situation falsely. In this respect it is close to sentimentality, a kinship that may explain why so many of our outstanding comedians (who are really humorists) have a fondness for antithetical lapses into orgies of the tearful. Their customary method of self-protection is the attitude of "happy stupidity" whereby the gravity of life simply fails to register; its importance is lost to them. The mimetics of this role is often completed by some *childish* quality of voice, as with Joe Penner, Gracie Allen, Eddie Cantor, the burbling Ed Wynn, the stutterers and the silent.

In the epic, the tragic, and the comic frames the element of *acceptance* is uppermost. We might also include here work in the spirit of the Horatian ode, the *carpe diem* attitude, which invites us to snatch whatever mild pleasures may be at hand, and call it a day. The lyric tends to fall into this bin, though often we may consider it with relation to the broader frames of adjustment, according to the ingredient it stresses in any particular case. As we turn towards the plaint or elegy, satire, burlesque and the grotesque, the element of *rejection* comes to the fore.

Negative Emphasis: the Elegy, or Plaint

Even here the distinction cannot be clearly maintained. William James, for instance, complained that Schopenhauer was *content* with his pessimism. He wanted a world that he could bark at. And unquestionably, once a man has *perfected* a technique of complaint, he is more at home with sorrow than he would be without it. He has developed an equipment, and the integrity of his character is best upheld by situations that enable him to use it. Otherwise, he would have to become either disintegrated or reborn. As a child, Augustine said, one learns to "avenge oneself by weeping"—and if one matures the same device by the use of adult material, one may paradoxically be said to have found a way of "accepting" life even while symbolizing its "rejection." In such cases, "acceptance" does come very close to "passiveness." The elegiac, the "wailing wall," may serve well for individual trickeries in one's relation to the obligations of struggle—but if it becomes organized as a collective movement, you may feel sure that a class of people will arise to "move in on" it, exploiting it to a point where more good reasons for complaint are provided, until the physical limits of the attitude are reached. Like humor, it is a frame that does not properly gauge the situation: when under its spell, one does not tend to size up his own resources accurately—but in contrast with humor, it really *spreads* the disproportion between the weakness of the self and the magnitude of the situation.

In *Some Versions of Pastoral,* a work that should be coupled with I. A. Richards' *Principles of Literary Criticism* and Caroline Spurgeon's *Shakespeare's Imagery* as the most important contributions to literary criticism in contemporary

England, William Empson proposes a definition of "pastoral" that would seem to fall on the bias across our categories of humor and elegy, with important ingredients of the heroic. Gray's "Elegy in a Country Church Yard," *The Beggar's Opera, The Vision of Piers Plowman,* and *Alice in Wonderland* are all analyzed as aspects of "pastoral." The heroic device operates, paradoxically, in the sympathetic treatment of *humble* people (like the Christian transvaluation of the pagan Percival legend whereby the "fool" becomes the "saint"). The lowly are pictured as the bearers of the true nobility, by the revolutionary "first shall be last and last shall be first" paradox. Children, fools, criminals, rogues, and simple rustics "turn slowly into Christ and ruler," as Empson says of the sorrowing Piers Plowman.

Empson's remarks on "ironic humility" are particularly relevant to our purposes:

> Ironic humility, whose simplest gambit is to say, 'I am not clever, educated, well born,' or what not (as if you had a low standard to judge by), and then to imply that your standards are so high in the matter that the person you are humbling yourself before is quite out of sight. This has an amusing likeness to pastoral; the important man classes himself among low men, and the effect is to raise his standards, not to lower them.

This is the "gentleman's" subtle form of boasting. He practices long and hard, he becomes an adept, he assures you that he is a veritable tyro—and then you play, and he beats you. In case you win, that also has been taken care of.[4]

Empson's analysis of Gray's reference to the flower

> born to blush unseen
> And waste its sweetness on the desert air

discloses the ways in which the poet, confronting the rise of

---

[4] One is reminded of the anecdote about the British prime minister. A member of his party, with a young son, asked the minister to find the son a position. The minister asked about the son's qualifications. "Well, he is very modest," said the father. "Modest!" exclaimed the minister; "What has he done to be modest about?" The anecdote draws its logic from the springs of "ironic humility."

the get-ahead philosophy that went with the mounting industrial-commercial pattern of England, provides resignation for the man who has not found a *carrière ouverte aux talents,* and yet would feel himself of good quality. It is "Marxist criticism" of a sort that few of our professional Marxists have discovered, though they may claim the virtue of having pressed Empson to break the confines of his earlier volume, *Seven Types of Ambiguity,* where the psychologism was of a different sort.

Satire

Satire is as confusing as the plaint. For the satirist attacks *in others* the weaknesses and temptations that are really *within himself.* The satiric projection could be charted roughly as follows: A and B have a private vice in common (both are kleptomaniacs, homosexuals, sadists, social climbers, or the like, in varying degrees of latency or patency). At the same time, on some platform of the public arena they are opponents (they belong to clashing forensic factions). A is a satirist. In excoriating B for his political views, A draws upon the imagery of the secret vice shared by both. A thereby *gratifies* and *punishes* the vice within himself. Is he whipped with his own lash? He is.

One cannot read great satirists like Swift or Juvenal without feeling this strategic ambiguity. We sense in them the Savonarola, who would exorcize his own vanities by building a fire of other people's vanities. Expertness in satiric practice makes good inventory almost impossible. Swift's aptitude at "projection" invited him to beat himself unmercifully, eventually with drastic results.

Wyndham Lewis, the compleat satirist of our day, would define satire as an approach "from without." To which we should agree, if we are permitted to add the reservation, "an approach *from without* to something *from within.*" In Lewis's case, there are symptoms to indicate that his excoriations arise from a suppressed fear of death, or, in other words, from religiosity frustrated by disbelief, though it must be admitted that our reasons for such diagnosis are tenuous. They are offered here for what they may be worth:

In Spender's book, *The Destructive Element,* you will find a comment on the analogy Lewis uses when advocating his thesis that satire is "from without," and that all good art is satire. Lewis says that art should not deal with the "intestines," but with the "ossature." Spender observes that even the "ossature" is internal, hence the very analogy that Lewis selects with a whole world of examples to pick from, is unfit. Now, if there is any justification to our contention that one may get cues about a writer's motives by noting the quality of the imagery he employs at strategic points, would there not be even greater justice in attributing significance to an image that bursts forth by an actual *discontinuity* in the logic? Lewis would observe "from without"—and illogically he picks something to observe that is *within;* namely: the skeleton. Our test might indicate the kind of drive behind his "eye-mindedness" and his hatred of "time-mindedness." For "eye-mindedness" enables him to *project* "the enemy," to look at it by subterfuge; but "time-mindedness" requires either the frank acceptance of death or the belief in immortality. To make the speculation a little less tenuous, recall that Tarr, when embracing a woman, is said to draw her "skull" to him, the quality of the imagery here suggesting a furtive linkage between heterosexual love and death.

True, there are other important ingredients here. The "opposite" of the ossature is the intestines, which gets us close to Swift's disgust with the excretions of the body—a disgust, as a significant quotation from Swift in Empson's *Some Versions of Pastoral* makes clear, that was also linked with sex, because of the way in which the body has economized in localizing the channels of these two functions. This sense of a union between love and filth was the essence of his working credo, that "everything spiritual and valuable has a gross and revolting parody, very similar to it, with the same name." If the "life within" equals the intestines, and the "life without" equals a deceptive projection of the skeleton, and the man's love of woman is secretly tied to both, maybe there *is* no way of making peace with the state of things. One is on the run, like Whitman, but without the "salute."

Burlesque

We might add one justification for externality that Lewis does not offer. Namely: if the state of the world and the criteria of art have gone to such a point that we are concerned primarily with the depiction of very despicable, forlorn, and dissipated people, the writer might very well protect himself by not imagining them with too great intimacy. For to picture them intimately, he must be one with them. Goethe has suggested that he was equipped as a writer by his ability to imagine himself committing every crime. Similarly, a writer who could imagine himself in the many humiliating roles that are in fashion today would, by this very ability, open himself to great risk. A purely *external* approach to such characters would protect him greatly. If he merely described their *behavior*, with depth in imagining the state of their *minds*, his superficiality would contribute to his comfort.

But that gets us to the matter of *burlesque*. It is our contention that Lewis's plea for the external is carried out, not in the satiric form, but in burlesque (and such related forms as polemic and caricature). Here the attack really is external— and for that reason, though we enjoy burlesque as an occasional dish, no critic has ever been inclined to select it as the *pièce de résistance* for a steady diet.

The writer of burlesque makes no attempt to get inside the psyche of his victim. Instead, he is content to select the externals of behavior, driving them to a "logical conclusion" that becomes their "reduction to absurdity." By program, he obliterates his victim's discriminations. He is "heartless." He converts every "perhaps" into a "positively." He deliberately suppresses any consideration of the "mitigating circumstances" that would put his subject in a better light. If the victim performs an act that would appear well when done slowly, he performs the same act at top speed; if the act is more appropriate for speed, he portrays it in slow motion. Hilariously, he converts a manner into a mannerism. The method of burlesque (polemic, caricature) is partial not only in the sense of *partisan,* but also in the sense of *incompleteness.* As such, it does not contain a well-rounded frame itself; we can use it for the ends of wisdom only insofar as we ourselves provide the ways of making allowances for it; we must not be merely *equal* to it, we must be enough *greater than* it to be able to "discount" what it says.

An enormous amount of early liberal pamphleteering was done within this mode. In fact, the very basis of classic liberal apologetics, the overemphasis upon freedom, was but a sober way of carrying out the burlesque genius. It *stressed* freedom, and sought to *smuggle* in restrictions. It cried for "rights," enjoying the strategic advantage of this invitation, without considering the corrective feature of ambivalence whereby "rights" also require their unpleasant reverse, "duties" or "obligations."

At the time of the French Revolution, when a "bill of rights" was being drawn, some members of the Assembly suggested that a "bill of obligations" be included to match them. The proposal was voted down by an overwhelming majority. Here the genius of neither tragedy nor comedy was at work, but the genius of burlesque.

The medieval scheme, so well-rounded *on paper,* had been made to *function* as the most *partial* of schemes, hence giving rise to a partial antithesis. But this burlesqued overemphasis has remained to plague us ever since, as we note today in the discomfitures of such a liberal as John Dewey who, in following the cues of classic liberalism, is still trying to introduce a plea for collective elements without admitting that a collective frame requires us to stress the *ambivalence* of rights and obligations (which would require a *formal admission* of strictures). A kindred hankering to preserve the liberal one-way system of apologetics is to be noted among the Southern agrarians, who want to make men "free" by making private property *inalienable,* ignoring the fact that the history of emancipation in Europe shows the *integral relation between freedom and alienation.* In "binding" the serf to the soil, feudalism also bound the soil to the serf, matching his "duties" with "rights" that were protected by custom. The liberal revolution "freed" him of his "duties" by alienating him from his "rights." Hence, for great numbers of the people, "freedom" functioned simply as "dispossession." Conversely, you cannot "repossess" without a corresponding pattern of obligation. "Freedom" is a truncated concept, an unintended *caricature* of human relations. Hence, the liberal who rates social organisms by its test alone is vowed to disillusionment. He will find that his ideals are too good for this world.[5]

[5] Significantly, it is the theoreticians behind Lewis's C.I.O. who are reintroducing into America the concept of ambivalence in property relationships. They are proceeding, roughly, as follows: Beginning with the recognition of the worker's obligations, they are insisting that these obligations be matched by rights. Hence, under the stimulus of their thinking, an economist writing in the daily press said recently: "Labor has a property right in skill, an ownership right in the job, an investment interest in income." Extend the concepts of property and ownership in this way, with institutions in keeping, and the classical coordinates of private ownership are automatically dissolved—somewhat as Schoenberg dissolved modulation in music by making compositions that were in *constant* modulation.

From *Attitudes Toward History* (2nd ed.; Los Altos, Calif.: Hermes Publications, 1959), pp. 34-56.

The Rhetoric of Hitler's "Battle"
(1939)

The appearance of *Mein Kampf* in unexpurgated translation has called forth far too many vandalistic comments. There are other ways of burning books than on the pyre—and the favorite method of the hasty reviewer is to deprive himself and his readers by inattention. I maintain that it is thoroughly vandalistic for the reviewer to content himself with the mere inflicting of a few symbolic wounds upon this book and its author, of an intensity varying with the resources of the reviewer and the time at his disposal. Hitler's "Battle" is exasperating, even nauseating; yet the fact remains: If the reviewer but knocks off a few adverse attitudinizings and calls it a day, with a guaranty in advance that his article will have a favorable reception among the decent members of our population, he is contributing more to our gratification than to our enlightenment.

Here is the testament of a man who swung a great people into his wake. Let us watch it carefully; and let us watch it, not merely to discover some grounds for prophesying what political move is to follow Munich, and what move to follow that move, etc.; let us try also to discover what kind of "medicine" this medicine-man has concocted, that we may know, with greater accuracy, exactly what to guard against, if we are to forestall the concocting of similar medicine in America.

Already, in many quarters of our country, we are "beyond" the stage where we are being saved from Nazism by our *virtues*. And fascist integration is being staved off, rather, by the *conflicts among our vices*. Our vices cannot get together in a grand united front of prejudices; and the result of this frustration, if or until they succeed in surmounting it, speaks, as the Bible might say, "in the name of" democracy. Hitler

95

found a panacea, a "cure for what ails you," a "snakeoil," that
made such sinister unifying possible within his own nation.
And he was helpful enough to put his cards face up on the
table, that we might examine his hands. Let us, then, for
God's sake, examine them. This book is the well of Nazi magic;
crude magic, but effective. A people trained in pragmatism
should want to inspect this magic.

I

Every movement that would recruit its followers from
among many discordant and divergent bands, must have some
spot towards which all roads lead. Each man may get there
in his own way, but it must be the one unifying center of
reference for all. Hitler considered this matter carefully, and
decided that this center must be not merely a centralizing hub
of *ideas,* but a mecca geographically located, towards which
all eyes could turn at the appointed hours of prayer (or, in
this case, the appointed hours of prayer-in-reverse, the hours
of vituperation). So he selected Munich, as the *materialization*
of his unifying panacea. As he puts it:

> The geo-political importance of a center of a movement cannot
> be overrated. Only the presence of such a center and of a place,
> bathed in the magic of a Mecca or a Rome, can at length give a
> movement that force which is rooted in the inner unity and in
> the recognition of a hand that represents this unity.

If a movement must have its Rome, it must also have its
devil. For as Russell pointed out years ago, an important ingredient of unity in the Middle Ages (an ingredient that long
did its unifying work despite the many factors driving towards
disunity) was the symbol of a *common enemy,* the Prince of
Evil himself. Men who can unite on nothing else can unite on
the basis of a foe shared by all. Hitler himself states the case
very succinctly:

As a whole, and at all times, the efficiency of the truly national leader consists primarily in preventing the division of the attention of a people, and always in concentrating it on a single enemy. The more uniformly the fighting will of a people is put into action, the greater will be the magnetic force of the movement and the more powerful the impetus of the blow. It is part of the genius of a great leader to make adversaries of different fields appear as always belonging to one category only, because to weak and unstable characters the knowledge that there are various enemies will lead only too easily to incipient doubts as to their own cause.

As soon as the wavering masses find themselves confronted with too many enemies, objectivity at once steps in, and the question is raised whether actually all the others are wrong and their own nation or their own movement alone is right.

Also with this comes the first paralysis of their own strength. Therefore, a number of essentially different enemies must always be regarded as one in such a way that in the opinion of the mass of one's own adherents the war is being waged against one enemy alone. This strengthens the belief in one's own cause and increases one's bitterness against the attacker.

As everyone knows, this policy was exemplified in his selection of an "international" devil, the "international Jew" (the Prince was international, universal, "catholic"). This *materialization* of a religious pattern is, I think, one terrifically effective weapon of propaganda in a period where religion has been progressively weakened by many centuries of capitalist materialism. You need but go back to the sermonizing of centuries to be reminded that religion had a powerful enemy long before organized atheism came upon the scene. Religion is based upon the "prosperity of poverty," upon the use of ways for converting our sufferings and handicaps into a good—but capitalism is based upon the prosperity of acquisitions, the only scheme of value, in fact, by which its proliferating store of gadgets could be sold, insofar as capitalism does not get so drastically in its own way that it can't sell its gadgets even after it has trained people to feel that human dignity, the "higher standard of living," could be attained only by such private accumulation.

So, we have, as unifying step No. I, the international devil materialized, in the visible, point-to-able form of people with a certain kind of "blood," a burlesque of contemporary neo-positivism's ideal of meaning, which insists upon a *material* reference.

Once Hitler has thus essentialized his enemy, all "proof" henceforth is automatic. If you point out the enormous amount of evidence to show that the Jewish worker is at odds with the "international Jew stock exchange capitalist," Hitler replies with one hundred per cent regularity: That is one more indication of the cunning with which the "Jewish plot" is being engineered. Or would you point to "Aryans" who do the same as his conspiratorial Jews? Very well; that is proof that the "Aryan" has been "seduced" by the Jew.

The sexual symbolism that runs through Hitler's book, lying in wait to draw upon the responses of contemporary sexual values, is easily characterized: Germany in dispersion is the "dehorned Siegfried." The masses are "feminine." As such, they desire to be led by a dominating male. This male, as orator, woos them—and, when he has won them, he commands them. The rival male, the villainous Jew, would on the contrary "seduce" them. If he succeeds, he poisons their blood by intermingling with them. Whereupon, by purely associative connections of ideas, we are moved into attacks upon syphilis, prostitution, incest, and other similar misfortunes, which are introduced as a kind of "musical" argument when he is on the subject of "bloodpoisoning" by intermarriage or, in its "spiritual" equivalent, by the infection of "Jewish" ideas, such as democracy.[1]

The "medicinal" appeal of the Jew as scapegoat operates from another angle. The middle class contains, within the mind of each member, a duality: its members simultaneously have a cult of money and a detestation of this cult. When capitalism is going well, this conflict is left more or less in abeyance. But when capitalism is balked, it comes to the fore.

[1] Hitler also strongly insists upon the total identification between leader and people. Thus, in wooing the people, he would in a round-about way be wooing himself. The thought might suggest how the Führer, dominating the feminine masses by his diction, would have an incentive to remain unmarried.

Hence, there is "medicine" for the "Aryan" members of the middle class in the projective device of the scapegoat, whereby the "bad" features can be allocated to the "devil," and one can "respect himself" by a distinction between "good" capitalism and "bad" capitalism, with those of a different lodge being the vessels of the "bad" capitalism. It is doubtless the "relief" of this solution that spared Hitler the necessity of explaining just how the "Jewish plot" was to work out. Nowhere does this book, which is so full of war plans, make the slightest attempt to explain the steps whereby the triumph of "Jewish Bolshevism," which destroys *all* finance, will be the triumph of *"Jewish"* finance. Hitler well knows the point at which his "elucidations" should rely upon the lurid alone.

The question arises, in those trying to gauge Hitler: Was his selection of the Jew, as his unifying devil-function, a purely calculating act? Despite the quotation I have already given, I believe that it was *not*. The vigor with which he utilized it, I think, derives from a much more complex state of affairs. It seems that, when Hitler went to Vienna, in a state close to total poverty, he genuinely suffered. He lived among the impoverished; and he describes his misery at the spectacle. He was *sensitive* to it; and his way of manifesting this sensitiveness impresses me that he is, at this point, wholly genuine, as with his wincing at the broken family relationships caused by alcoholism, which he in turn relates to impoverishment. During this time he began his attempts at political theorizing; and his disturbance was considerably increased by the skill with which Marxists tied him into knots. One passage in particular gives you reason, reading between the lines, to believe that the dialecticians of the class struggle, in their skill at blasting his muddled speculations, put him into a state of uncertainty that was finally "solved" by rage:

The more I argued with them, the more I got to know their dialectics. First, they counted on the ignorance of their adversary; then, when there was no way out, they themselves pretended stupidity. If all this was of no avail, they refused to understand or they changed the subject when driven into a corner; they brought up truisms, but they immediately transferred their acceptance to quite different subjects, and, if attacked again, they gave way and pretended to know nothing exactly. Wherever one attacked one of these prophets, one's hands seized slimy jelly; it slipped through one's fingers only to collect again in the next moment. If one smote one of them so thoroughly that, with the bystanders watching, he could but agree, and if one thus thought he had advanced at least one step, one was greatly astonished the following day. The Jew did not in the least remember the day before, he continued to talk in the same old strain as if nothing had happened, and if indignantly confronted, he pretended to be astonished and could not remember anything except that his assertions had already been proved true the day before.

Often I was stunned.

One did not know what to admire more: their glibness of tongue or their skill in lying.

I gradually began to hate them.

At this point, I think, he is tracing the *spontaneous* rise of his anti-Semitism. He tells how, once he had discovered the "cause" of the misery about him, he could *confront it*. Where he had had to avert his eyes, he could now *positively welcome* the scene. Here his drastic structure of *acceptance* was being formed. He tells of the "internal happiness" that descended upon him.

This was the time in which the greatest change I was ever to experience took place in me.

From a feeble cosmopolite I turned into a fanatical anti-Semite,

and thence we move, by one of those associational tricks which he brings forth at all strategic moments, into a vision of the end of the world—out of which in turn he emerges with his slogan: "I am acting in the sense of the Almighty Creator: *By warding off Jews I am fighting for the Lord's work*" (italics his).

He talks of this transition as a period of "double life," a struggle of "reason" and "reality" against his "heart." [2] It was

[2] Other aspects of the career symbolism: Hitler's book begins: "Today I consider it my good fortune that Fate designated Braunau on the Inn as the place of my birth. For this small town is situated on the border between those two German States, the reunion of which seems, at least to us of the younger generation, a task to be furthered with every means

as "bitter" as it was "blissful." And finally, it was "reason" that won! Which prompts us to note that those who attack Hitlerism as a cult of the irrational should emend their statements to this extent: irrational it is, but it is carried on under the *slogan* of "Reason." Similarly, his cult of war is developed "in the name of" humility, love, and peace. Judged on a quantitative basis, Hitler's book certainly falls under the classification of hate. Its venom is everywhere, its charity is sparse. But the rationalized family tree for this hate situates it in "Aryan love." Some deep-probing German poets, whose work adumbrated the Nazi movement, did gravitate towards thinking *in the name of* war, irrationality, and hate. But Hitler was not among them. After all, when it is so easy to draw a doctrine of war out of a doctrine of peace, why should the astute politician do otherwise, particularly when Hitler has slung together his doctrines, without the slightest effort at logical symmetry? Furthermore, Church thinking always got to its wars in Hitler's

---

our lives long," an indication of his "transitional" mind, what Wordsworth might have called the "borderer." He neglects to give the date of his birth, 1889, which is supplied by the editors. Again there is a certain "correctness" here, as Hitler was not "born" until many years later —but he does give the exact date of war wounds, which were indeed formative. During his early years in Vienna and Munich, he forgoes protest, on the grounds that he is "nameless." And when his party is finally organized and effective, he stresses the fact that his "nameless" period is over (i.e., he has shaped himself an identity). When reading in an earlier passage of his book some generalizations to the effect that one should not crystalize his political views until he is thirty, I made a note: "See what Hitler does at thirty." I felt sure that, though such generalizations may be dubious as applied to people as a whole, they must, given the Hitler type of mind (with his complete identification between himself and his followers), be valid statements about himself. One *should* do what he *did*. The hunch was verified: about the age of thirty, Hitler, in a group of seven, began working with the party that was to conquer Germany. I trace these steps particularly because I believe that the orator who has a strong sense of his own "rebirth" has this to draw upon when persuading his audiences that he is offering them the way to a "new life." However, I see no categorical objection to this attitude; its menace derives solely from the values in which it is exemplified. They may be wholesome or unwholesome. If they are unwholesome, but backed by conviction, the basic sincerity of the conviction acts as a sound virtue to reinforce a vice—and this combination is the most disastrous one that a people can encounter in a demagogue.

"sounder" manner; and the patterns of Hitler's thought are a bastardized or caricatured version of religious thought.

I spoke of Hitler's fury at the dialectics of those who opposed him when his structure was in the stage of scaffolding. From this we may move to another tremendously important aspect of his theory: his attack upon the *parliamentary*. For it is again, I submit, an important aspect of his medicine, in its function as medicine for him personally and as medicine for those who were later to identify themselves with him.

There is a "problem" in the parliament—and nowhere was this problem more acutely in evidence than in the prewar Vienna that was to serve as Hitler's political schooling. For the parliament, at its best, is a "babel" of voices. There is the wrangle of men representing interests lying awkwardly on the bias across one another, sometimes opposing, sometimes vaguely divergent. Morton Prince's psychiatric study of "Miss Beauchamp," the case of a woman split into several sub-personalities at odds with one another, variously combining under hypnosis, and frequently in turmoil, is the allegory of a democracy fallen upon evil days. The parliament of the Habsburg Empire just prior to its collapse was an especially drastic instance of such disruption, such vocal diaspora, with movements that would reduce one to a disintegrated mass of fragments if he attempted to encompass the totality of its discordancies. So Hitler, suffering under the alienation of poverty and confusion, yearning for some integrative core, came to take this parliament as the basic symbol of all that he would move away from. He damned the tottering Habsburg Empire as a "State of Nationalities." The many conflicting voices of the spokesmen of the many political blocs arose from the fact that various separationist movements of a nationalistic sort had arisen within a Catholic imperial structure formed prior to the nationalistic emphasis and slowly breaking apart under its development. So, you had this Babel of voices; and, by the method of associative mergers, *using ideas as imagery*, it became tied up, in the Hitler rhetoric, with "Babylon," Vienna as the city of poverty, prostitution, immorality, coalitions, half-measures, incest, democracy (i.e., majority rule leading to "lack of personal responsibility"), death, internationalism, seduction, and anything else of thumbs-down sort the associative enterprise cared to add on this side of the balance.

Hitler's way of treating the parliamentary babel, I am sorry to say, was at one important point not much different from that of the customary editorial in our own newspapers. Every conflict among the parliamentary spokesmen represents a corresponding conflict among the material interests of the groups for whom they are speaking. But Hitler did not discuss the babel from this angle. He discussed it on a purely *symptomatic* basis. The strategy of our orthodox press, in thus ridiculing the cacophonous verbal output of Congress, is obvious: by thus centering attack upon the *symptoms* of business conflict, as they reveal themselves on the dial of political wrangling, and leaving the underlying cause, the business conflicts themselves, out of the case, they can gratify the very public they would otherwise alienate: namely, the businessmen who are the activating members of their reading public. Hitler, however, went them one better. For not only did he stress the purely *symptomatic* attack here. He proceeded to search for the "cause." And this "cause," of course, he derived from his medicine, his racial theory by which he could give a noneconomic interpretation of a phenomenon economically engendered.

Here again is where Hitler's corrupt use of religious patterns comes to the fore. Church thought, being primarily concerned with matters of the "personality," with problems of moral betterment, naturally, and I think rightly, stresses as a necessary feature, the act of will upon the part of the individual. Hence its resistance to a purely "environmental" account of human ills. Hence its emphasis upon the "person." Hence its proneness to seek a noneconomic explanation of economic phenomena. Hitler's proposal of a noneconomic "cause" for the disturbances thus had much to recommend it from this angle. And, as a matter of fact, it was Lueger's Christian-Social Party in Vienna that taught Hitler the tactics of tying up a program of social betterment with an anti-Semitic "unifier." The two parties that he carefully studied at that time were this Catholic faction and Schoenerer's Pan-German group. And his analysis of their attainments and shortcomings, from the standpoint of demagogic efficacy, is an extremely astute piece of work, revealing how carefully this man used the current situation in Vienna as an experimental laboratory for the maturing of his plans.

His unification device, we may summarize, had the following important features:

(1) Inborn dignity. In both religious and humanistic patterns of thought, a "natural born" dignity of man is stressed. And this categorical dignity is considered to be an attribute of *all* men, if they will but avail themselves of it, by right thinking and right living. But Hitler gives this ennobling attitude an ominous twist by his theories of race and nation, whereby the "Aryan" is elevated above all others by the innate endowment of his blood, while other "races," in particular Jews and Negroes, are innately inferior. This sinister secularized revision of Christian theology thus puts the sense of dignity upon a fighting basis, requiring the conquest of "inferior races." After the defeat of Germany in the World War, there were especially strong emotional needs that this compensatory doctrine of an *inborn* superiority could gratify.

(2) *Projection* device. The "curative" process that comes with the ability to hand over one's ills to a scapegoat, thereby getting purification by dissociation. This was especially medicinal, since the sense of frustration leads to a self-questioning. Hence if one can hand over his infirmities to a vessel, or "cause," outside the self, one can battle an external enemy instead of battling an enemy within. And the greater one's internal inadequacies, the greater amount of evils one can load upon the back of "the enemy." This device is furthermore given a semblance of reason because the individual properly realizes that he is not alone responsible for his condition. There *are* inimical factors in the scene itself. And he wants to have them "placed," preferably in a way that would require

a minimum change in the ways of thinking to which he had been accustomed. This was especially appealing to the middle class, who were encouraged to feel that they could conduct their businesses without any basic change whatever, once the businessmen of a different "race" were eliminated.

(3) *Symbolic rebirth.* Another aspect of the two features already noted. The projective device of the scapegoat, coupled with the Hitlerite doctrine of inborn racial superiority, provides its followers with a "positive" view of life. They can again get the feel of *moving forward,* towards a *goal* (a promissory feature of which Hitler makes much). In Hitler, as the group's prophet, such rebirth involved a symbolic change of lineage. Here, above all, we see Hitler giving a malign twist to a benign aspect of Christian thought. For whereas the Pope, in the familistic pattern of thought basic to the Church, stated that the Hebrew prophets were the *spiritual ancestors* of Christianity, Hitler uses this same mode of thinking in reverse. He renounces this "ancestry" in a "materialistic" way by voting himself and the members of his lodge a different "bloodstream" from that of the Jews.

(4) *Commercial use.* Hitler obviously here had something to sell—and it was but a question of time until he sold it (i.e., got financial backers for his movement). For it provided a *noneconomic interpretation of economic ills.* As such, it served with maximum efficiency in deflecting the attention from the economic factors involved in modern conflict; hence by attacking "Jew finance" instead of *finance,* it could stimulate an enthusiastic movement that left "Aryan" finance in control.

Never once, throughout his book, does Hitler deviate from such a formula. Invariably, he ends his diatribes against contemporary economic ills by a shift into an insistence that we must get to the "true" cause, which is centered in "race." The "Aryan" is "constructive"; the Jew is "destructive"; and the "Aryan," to continue his *construction,* must *destroy* the Jewish *destruction.* The Aryan, as the vessel of *love,* must *hate* the Jewish *hate.*

Perhaps the most enterprising use of his method is in his

chapter, "The Causes of the Collapse," where he refuses to consider Germany's plight as in any basic way connected with the consequences of war. Economic factors, he insists, are "only of second or even third importance," but "political, ethical-moral, as well as factors of blood and race, are of the first importance." His rhetorical steps are especially interesting here, in that he begins by seeming to flout the national susceptibilities: "The military defeat of the German people is not an undeserved catastrophe, but rather a deserved punishment by eternal retribution." He then proceeds to present the military collapse as but a "consequence of moral poisoning, visible to all, the consequence of a decrease in the instinct of self-preservation . . . which had already begun to undermine the foundations of the people and the Reich many years before." This moral decay derived from "a sin against the blood and the degradation of the race," so its innerness was an outerness after all: the Jew, who thereupon gets saddled with a vast amalgamation of evils, among them being capitalism, democracy, pacifism, journalism, poor housing, modernism, big cities, loss of religion, half measures, ill health, and weakness of the monarch.

2

Hitler had here another important psychological ingredient to play upon. If a State is in economic collapse (and his theories, tentatively taking shape in the prewar Vienna, were but developed with greater efficiency in postwar Munich), you cannot possibly derive dignity from economic stability. Dignity must come first—and if you possess it, and implement it, from it may follow its economic counterpart. There is much justice to this line of reasoning, so far as it goes. A people in collapse, suffering under economic frustration and the defeat of nationalistic aspirations, with the very midrib of their integrative efforts (the army) in a state of dispersion, have little other than some "spiritual" basis to which they could refer their nationalistic dignity. Hence, the categorical dignity of superior race was a perfect recipe for the situation. It was "spiritual" insofar as it was "above" crude economic "interests," but it was "materialized" at the psychologically "right" spot in that "the enemy" was something you could *see*.

Furthermore, you had the desire for unity, such as a discussion of class conflict, on the basis of conflicting interests, could not satisfy. The yearning for unity is so great that people are always willing to meet you halfway if you will give it to them by fiat, by flat statement, regardless of the facts. Hence, Hitler consistently refused to consider internal political conflicts on the basis of conflicting interests. Here again, he could draw upon a religious pattern, by insisting upon a *personal* statement of the relation between classes, the relation between leaders and followers, each group in its way fulfilling the same commonalty of interests, as the soldiers and captains of an army share a common interest in victory. People so dislike the idea of internal division that, where there is a real internal division, their dislike can easily be turned against the man or group who would so much as *name* it, let alone proposing to act upon it. Their natural and justified resentment against internal division itself, is turned against the diagnostician who states it as a *fact*. This diagnostician, it is felt, is the *cause* of the disunity he named.

Cutting in from another angle, therefore, we note how two sets of equations were built up, with Hitler attaining a coalescence of *ideas* the way a poet might combine *images*. On the one side, were the ideas, or images, of disunity, centering in the parliamentary wrangle of the Habsburg "State of Nationalities." This was offered as the antithesis of German nationality, which was presented in the curative imagery of unity, focused upon the glories of the Prussian Reich, with its mecca now moved to "folkish" Vienna. For though Hitler at first attacked the many "folkish" movements, with their hankerings after a kind of Wagnerian mythology of Germanic origins, he subsequently took "folkish" as a basic word by which to conjure. It was, after all, another noneconomic basis of reference. At first we find him objecting to "those who drift about with the word 'folkish' on their caps," and asserting that "such a Babel of opinions cannot serve as the basis of a political fighting movement." But later he seems to have realized, as he well should, that its vagueness was a major point in its favor. So it was incorporated in the grand coalition of his ideational imagery, or imagistic ideation; and Chapter XI ends with the vision of "a State which represents not a mechanism of economic considerations and interests, alien to the people, but a folkish organism."

So, as against the disunity equations, already listed briefly in our discussion of his attacks upon the parliamentary, we get a contrary purifying set; the wrangle of the parliamentary is to be stilled by the giving of *one* voice to the people, this to be the "inner voice" of Hitler, made uniform throughout the German boundaries, as leader and people were completely identified with each other. In sum: Hitler's inner voice, equals leader-people identification, equals unity, equals Reich, equals the mecca of Munich, equals plow, equals sword, equals work, equals war, equals army as midrib, equals responsibility (the personal responsibility of the absolute ruler), equals sacrifice, equals the theory of "German democracy" (the free popular choice of the leader, who then accepts the responsibility, and demands absolute obedience in exchange for his sacrifice), equals love (with the masses as feminine), equals idealism, equals obedience to nature, equals race, nation.[3]

[3] One could carry out the equations further, on both the disunity and unity side. In the esthetic field, for instance, we have expressionism on the thumbs-down side, as against esthetic hygiene on the thumbs-up side. This again is a particularly ironic moment in Hitler's strategy. For the expressionist movement was unquestionably a symptom of unhealthiness. It reflected the increasing alienation that went with the movement towards world war and the disorganization after the world war. It was "lost," vague in identity, a drastically accurate reflection of the response to material confusion, a pathetic attempt by sincere artists to make their wretchedness bearable at least to the extent that comes of giving it expression. And it attained its height during the period of wild inflation, when the capitalist world, which bases its morality of work and savings upon the soundness of its money structure, had this last prop of stability removed. The anguish, in short,

And, of course, the two keystones of these opposite equations were Aryan "heroism" and "sacrifice" vs. Jewish "cunning" and "arrogance." Here again we get an astounding caricature of religious thought. For Hitler presents the concept of "Aryan" superiority in terms of nothing less than "Aryan humility." This "humility" is extracted by a very delicate process that requires, I am afraid, considerable "good will" on the part of the reader who would follow it:

The Church, we may recall, had proclaimed an integral relationship between Divine Law and Natural Law. Natural Law was the expression of the Will of God. Thus, in the Middle Ages, it was a result of natural law, working through tradition, that some people were serfs and other people nobles. And every good member of the Church was "obedient" to this law. Everybody resigned himself to it. Hence, the serf resigned himself to his poverty, and the noble resigned himself to his riches. The monarch resigned himself to his position as representative of the people. And at times the Churchmen resigned themselves to the need of trying to represent the people instead. And the pattern was made symmetrical by the consideration that each traditional "right" had its corresponding "obligations." Similarly, the Aryan doctrine is a doctrine of resignation, hence of humility. It is in accordance with the laws of nature that the "Aryan blood" is superior to all other bloods. Also, the "law of the survival of the fittest" is God's law, working through natural law. Hence, if the Aryan blood has been vested with the awful responsibility of its inborn superiority, the bearers of this "culture-creating" blood must resign themselves to struggle in behalf of its triumph. Otherwise, the laws of God have been disobeyed, with human decadence as a result. We must fight, he says, in order to "deserve to be alive." The Aryan "obeys" nature. It is only "Jewish arrogance" that thinks of "conquering" nature by democratic ideals of equality.

---

reflected precisely the kind of disruption that made people *ripe* for a Hitler. It was the antecedent in a phrase of which Hitlerism was the consequent. But by thundering against this *symptom* he could gain persuasiveness, though attacking the very *foreshadowings of himself.*

This picture has some nice distinctions worth following. The major virtue of the Aryan race was its instinct for self-preservation (in obedience to natural law). But the major vice of the Jew was his instinct for self-preservation; for, if he did not have this instinct to a maximum degree, he would not be the "perfect" enemy—that is, he wouldn't be strong enough to account for the ubiquitousness and omnipotence of his conspiracy in destroying the world to become its master.

How, then, are we to distinguish between the benign instinct of self-preservation at the roots of Aryanism, and the malign instinct of self-preservation at the roots of Semitism? We shall distinguish thus: The Aryan self-preservation is based upon *sacrifice,* the sacrifice of the individual to the group, hence, militarism, army discipline, and one big company union. But Jewish self-preservation is based upon individualism, which attains its cunning ends by the exploitation of peace. How, then, can such arrant individualists concoct the world-wide plot? By the help of their "herd instinct." By their sheer "herd instinct" individualists can band together for a common end. They have no real solidarity, but unite opportunistically to seduce the Aryan. Still, that brings up another technical problem. For we have been hearing much about the importance of the *person.* We have been told how, by the "law of the survival of the fittest," there is a sifting of people on the basis of their individual capacities. We even have a special chapter of pure Aryanism: "The Strong Man is Mightiest Alone." Hence, another distinction is necessary: The Jew represents individualism; the Aryan represents "super-individualism."

I had thought, when coming upon the "Strong Man is Mightiest Alone" chapter, that I was going to find Hitler at his weakest. Instead, I found him at his strongest. (I am not referring to *quality,* but to *demagogic effectiveness.*) For the chapter is not at all, as you might infer from the title, done in a "rise of Adolph Hitler" manner. Instead, it deals with the Nazis' gradual absorption of the many disrelated "folkish" groups. And it is managed throughout by means of a spontaneous identification between leader and people. Hence, the Strong Man's "aloneness" is presented as a *public* attribute, in terms of tactics for the struggle against the *Party's* dismemberment under the pressure of rival saviors. There is no explicit talk of Hitler at all. And it is simply *taken for granted* that *his* leadership is the norm, and all other leaderships the abnorm. There is no "philosophy of the superman," in Nietzschean cast. Instead, Hitler's blandishments so integrate leader and people, commingling them so inextricably, that the politician does not even present himself as candidate. Somehow, the battle is over already, the decision has been made. "German democracy" has chosen. And the deployments of politics are, you might say, the chartings of Hitler's private mind translated into the vocabulary of nationalistic events. He says *what he thought* in terms of *what parties did*.

Here, I think, we see the distinguishing quality of Hitler's method as an instrument of persuasion, with reference to the question whether Hitler is sincere or deliberate, whether his vision of the omnipotent conspirator has the drastic honesty of paranoia or the sheer shrewdness of a demagogue trained in *Realpolitik* of the Machiavellian sort.[4] Must we choose? Or may we not, rather, replace the "either—or" with a "both—

⁴ I should not want to use the word "Machiavellian," however, without offering a kind of apology to Machiavelli. It seems to me that Machiavelli's *Prince* has more to be said in extenuation than is usually said of it. Machiavelli's strategy, as I see it, was something like this: He accepted the values of the Renaissance rule as a *fact*. That is: whether you like these values or not, they were there and operating, and it was useless to try persuading the ambitious ruler to adopt other values, such as those of the Church. These men believed in the cult of material power, and they had the power to implement their beliefs. With so much as "the given," could anything in the way of benefits for the people be salvaged? Machiavelli evolved a typical "Machiavellian" argument in favor of popular benefits, on the basis of the prince's own scheme of values. That is: the ruler, to attain the maximum strength, requires the backing of the populace. That this backing be as effective as possible, the populace should be made as strong as possible. And that the populace be as strong as possible, they should be well treated. Their gratitude would further repay itself in the form of increased loyalty.

It was Machiavelli's hope that, for this roundabout project, he would be rewarded with a well-paying office in the prince's administrative bureaucracy.

and"? Have we not by now offered grounds enough for our contention that Hitler's sinister powers of persuasion derive from the fact that he spontaneously evolved his "cure-all" in response to inner necessities?

3

So much, then, was "spontaneous." It was further channelized into the anti-Semitic pattern by the incentives he derived from the Catholic Christian-Social Party in Vienna itself. Add, now, the step into *criticism*. Not criticism in the "parliamentary" sense of doubt, of hearkening to the opposition and attempting to mature a policy in the light of counter-policies; but the "unified" kind of criticism that simply seeks for conscious ways of making one's position more "efficient," more thoroughly itself. This is the kind of criticism at which Hitler was an adept. As a result, he could *spontaneously* turn to a scapegoat mechanism, and he could, by conscious planning, perfect the symmetry of the solution towards which he had spontaneously turned.

This is the meaning of Hitler's diatribes against "objectivity." "Objectivity" is interference-criticism. What Hitler wanted was the kind of criticism that would be a pure and simple coefficient of power, enabling him to go most effectively in the direction he had chosen. And the "inner voice" of which he speaks would henceforth dictate to him the greatest amount of realism, as regards the tactics of efficiency. For instance, having decided that the masses required certainty, and simple certainty, quite as he did himself, he later worked out a 25-point program as the platform of his National Socialist German Workers Party. And he resolutely refused to change one single item in this program, even for purposes of "improvement." He felt that the *fixity* of the platform was more important for propagandistic purposes than any revision of his slogans could be, even though the revisions in themselves had much to be said in their favor. The astounding thing is that, although such an attitude gave good cause to doubt the Hitlerite promises, he could explicitly explain his tactics in his book and still employ them without loss of effectiveness.[5]

Hitler also tells of his technique in speaking, once the Nazi party had become effectively organized, and had its army of guards, or bouncers, to maltreat hecklers and throw them from the hall. He would, he recounts, fill his speech with *provocative* remarks, whereat his bouncers would promptly swoop down in flying formation, with swinging fists, upon anyone whom these provocative remarks provoked to answer. The efficiency of Hitlerism is the efficiency of the one voice, implemented throughout a total organization. The trinity of government which he finally offers is: *popularity* of the leader, *force* to back the popularity, and popularity and force maintained together long enough to become backed by a *tradition.* Is such thinking spontaneous or deliberate—or is it not rather both?[6]

[5] On this point Hitler reasons as follows: "Here, too, one can learn from the Catholic Church. Although its structure of doctrines in many instances collides, quite unnecessarily, with exact science and research, yet it is unwilling to sacrifice even one little syllable of its dogmas. It has rightly recognized that its resistibility does not lie in a more or less great adjustment to the scientific results of the moment, which in reality are always changing, but rather in a strict adherence to dogmas, once laid down, which alone give the entire structure the character of creed. Today, therefore, the Catholic Church stands firmer than ever. One can prophesy that in the same measure in which the appearances flee, the Church itself, as the resting pole in the flight of appearances, will gain more and more blind adherence."

[6] Hitler also paid great attention to the conditions under which political oratory is most effective. He sums up thus:

"All these cases involve encroachments upon man's freedom of will. This applies, of course, most of all to meetings to which people with a contrary orientation of will are coming, and who now have to be won for new intentions. It seems that in the morning and even during the day men's will power revolts with highest energy against an attempt at being forced under another's will and another's opinion. In the evening, however, they succumb more easily to the dominating force of a stronger will. For truly every such meeting presents a wrestling match between two opposed forces. The superior oratorical talent of a domineering apostolic nature will now succeed more easily in winning for the new will people who themselves have in turn experienced a weakening of their force of resistance in the most natural way, than people who still

Freud has given us a succinct paragraph that bears upon the spontaneous aspect of Hitler's persecution mania. (A persecution mania, I should add, different from the pure product in that it was constructed of *public* materials; all the ingredients Hitler stirred into his brew were already rife, with spokesmen and bands of followers, before Hitler "took them over." Both the prewar and postwar periods were dotted with saviors, of nationalistic and "folkish" cast. This proliferation was analogous to the swarm of barter schemes and currency-tinkering that burst loose upon the United States after the crash of 1929. Also, the commercial availability of Hitler's politics was, in a low sense of the term, a *public* qualification, removing it from the realm of "pure" paranoia, where the sufferer develops a wholly *private* structure of interpretations.)

I cite from *Totem and Taboo:*

Another trait in the attitude of primitive races towards their rulers recalls a mechanism which is universally present in mental disturbances, and is openly revealed in the so-called delusions of persecution. Here the importance of a particular person is extraordinarily heightened and his omnipotence is raised to the improbable in order to make it easier to attribute to him responsibility for everything painful which happens to the patient. Savages really do not act differently towards their rulers when they ascribe to them power over rain and shine, wind and weather, and then dethrone them or kill them because nature has disappointed their expectation of a good hunt or a ripe harvest. The prototype which the paranoiac reconstructs in his persecution mania is found in the relation of the child to its father. Such omnipotence is regularly attributed to the father in the imagination of the son, and distrust of the father has been shown to be intimately connected with the heightened esteem for him. When a paranoiac names a person of his acquaintance as his "persecutor," he thereby elevates him to the paternal succession and brings him under conditions which enable him to make him responsible for all the misfortune which he experiences.

---

have full command of the energies of their minds and their will power.

"The same purpose serves also the artificially created and yet mysterious dusk of the Catholic churches, the burning candles, incense, censers, etc."

I have already proposed my modifications of this account when discussing the symbolic change of lineage connected with Hitler's project of a "new way of life." Hitler is symbolically changing from the "spiritual ancestry" of the Hebrew prophets to the "superior" ancestry of "Aryanism," and has given his story a kind of bastardized modernization, along the lines of naturalistic, materialistic "science," by his fiction of the special "bloodstream." He is voting himself a new identity (something contrary to the wrangles of the Habsburg Babylon, a soothing national unity); whereupon the vessels of the old identity become a "bad" father, i.e., the persecutor. It is not hard to see how, as his enmity becomes implemented by the backing of an organization, the role of "persecutor" is transformed into the role of persecuted, as he sets out with his like-minded band to "destroy the destroyer."

Were Hitler simply a poet, he might have written a work with an anti-Semitic turn, and let it go at that. But Hitler, who began as a student of painting, and later shifted to architecture, himself treats his political activities as an extension of his ambitions. He remained, in his own eyes, an "architect," building a "folkish" State that was to match, in political materials, the "folkish" architecture of Munich.

We might consider the matter this way (still trying, that is, to make precise the relationship between the drastically sincere and the deliberately scheming): Do we not know of many authors who seem, as they turn from the role of citizen to the role of spokesman, to leave one room and enter another? Or who has not, on occasion, talked with a man in private conversation, and then been almost startled at the transformation this man undergoes when addressing a public audience? And I know persons today, who shift between the writing of items in the class of academic, philosophic speculation to items of political pamphleteering, and whose entire style and method changes with this change of role. In their academic manner, they are cautious, painstaking, eager to present all significant aspects of the case they are considering; but when they turn to political pamphleteering, they hammer forth with vituperation, they systematically misrepresent the position of their opponent, they go into a kind of political trance, in which, during its throes, they throb like a locomotive; and behold, a moment later, the mediumistic state is abandoned, and they are the most moderate of men.

Now, one will find few pages in Hitler that one could call "moderate." But there are many pages in which he gauges resistances and opportunities with the "rationality" of a skilled advertising man planning a new sales campaign. Politics, he says, must be sold like soap—and soap is not sold in a trance. But he did have the experience of his trance, in the "exaltation" of his anti-Semitism. And later, as he became a successful orator (he insists that revolutions are made solely by the power of the spoken word), he had this "poetic" role to draw upon, plus the great relief it provided as a way of slipping from the burden of logical analysis into the pure "spirituality" of vituperative prophecy. What more natural, therefore, than that a man so insistent upon unification would integrate this mood with less ecstatic moments, particularly when he had found the followers and the backers that put a price, both spiritual and material, upon such unifications?

Once this happy "unity" is under way, one has a "logic" for the development of a method. One knows when to "spiritualize" a material issue, and when to "materialize" a spiritual one. Thus, when it is a matter of materialistic interests that cause a conflict between employer and employee, Hitler here disdainfully shifts to a high moral plane. He is "above" such low concerns. Everything becomes a matter of "sacrifices" and "personality." It becomes crass to treat employers and employees as different *classes* with a corresponding difference in the classification of their interests. Instead, relations between employer and employee must be on the "personal" basis of leader and follower, and "whatever may have a divisive effect in national life should be given a unifying effect through the army." When talking of national rivalries, however, he makes a very shrewd materialistic gauging of Britain and France with relation to Germany. France, he says, desires the

"Balkanization of Germany" (i.e., its breakup into separationist movements—the "disunity" theme again) in order to maintain commercial hegemony on the continent. But Britain desires the "Balkanization of *Europe*," hence would favor a fairly strong and unified Germany, to use as a counterweight against French hegemony. *German* nationality, however, is unified by the *spiritual* quality of Aryanism (that would produce the national organization via the Party) while this in turn is *materialized* in the myth of the bloodstream.

What are we to learn from Hitler's book? For one thing, I believe that he has shown, to a very disturbing degree, the power of endless repetition. Every circular advertising a Nazi meeting had, at the bottom, two slogans: "Jews not admitted" and "War victims free." And the substance of Nazi propaganda was built about these two "complementary" themes. He describes the power of spectacle; insists that mass meetings are the fundamental way of giving the individual the sense of being protectively surrounded by a movement, the sense of "community." He also drops one wise hint that I wish the American authorities would take in treating Nazi gatherings. He says that the presence of a special Nazi guard, in Nazi uniforms, was of great importance in building up, among the followers, a tendency to place the center of authority in the Nazi party. I believe that we should take him at his word here, but use the advice in reverse, by insisting that, where Nazi meetings are to be permitted, they be policed by the authorities alone, and that uniformed Nazi guards to enforce the law be prohibited.

And is it possible that an equally important feature of appeal was not so much in the repetitiousness per se, but in the fact that, by means of it, Hitler provided a "world view" for people who had previously seen the world but piecemeal? Did not much of his lure derive, once more, from the *bad* filling of a good need? Are not those who insist upon a purely *planless* working of the market asking people to accept far too slovenly a scheme of human purpose, a slovenly scheme that can be accepted so long as it operates with a fair degree of satis-

faction, but becomes abhorrent to the victims of its disarray?
Are they not then psychologically ready for a rationale, *any* rationale, if it but offer them some specious "universal" explanation? Hence, I doubt whether the appeal was in the sloganizing
element alone (particularly as even slogans can only be ham-
mered home, in speech after speech, and two or three hours
at a stretch, by endless variations on the themes). And Hitler
himself somewhat justifies my interpretation by laying so much
stress upon the *half measures* of the middle-class politicians,
and the contrasting *certainty* of his own methods. He was not
offering people a *rival* world view; rather, he was offering a
world view to people who had no other to pit against it.

As for the basic Nazi trick: the "curative" unification by a
fictitious devil-function, gradually made convincing by the
sloganizing repetitiousness of standard advertising technique
—the opposition must be as unwearying in the attack upon
it. It may well be that people, in their human frailty, require
an enemy as well as a goal. Very well: Hitlerism itself has
provided us with such an enemy—and the clear example of
its operation is guaranty that we have, in Hitler and all he
stands for, no purely fictitious "devil-function" made to look
like a world menace by rhetorical blandishments, but a reality
whose ominousness is clarified by the record of its conduct
to date. In selecting his brand of doctrine as our "scapegoat,"
and in tracking down its equivalents in America, we shall be
at the very center of accuracy. The Nazis themselves had made
the task of clarification easier. Add to them Japan and Italy,
and you have *case histories* of fascism for those who might
find it more difficult to approach an understanding of its imperialistic drives by a vigorously economic explanation.

But above all, I believe, we must make it apparent that
Hitler appeals by relying upon a bastardization of fundamentally religious patterns of thought. In this, if properly
presented, there is no slight to religion. There is nothing in
religion proper that requires a fascist state. There is much in
religion, when misused, that does lead to a fascist state. There
is a Latin proverb, *Corruptio optimi pessima,* "the corruption

of the best is the worst." And it is the corruptors of religion who are a major menace to the world today, in giving the profound patterns of religious thought a crude and sinister distortion.

From *The Philosophy of Literary Form: Studies in Symbolic Action* (2nd ed.; New York: Vintage Books, 1957), pp. 164-188.

Ritual Drama as Hub
(*1941*)

The general perspective that is interwoven with our methodology of analysis might be summarily characterized as a *theory of drama*. We propose to take *ritual drama* as the Urform, the "hub," with all other aspects of *human* action treated as spokes radiating from this hub. That is, the social sphere is considered in terms of situations and acts, in contrast with the physical sphere, which is considered in mechanistic terms, idealized as a flat cause-and-effect or stimulus-and-response relationship. Ritual drama is considered as the culminating form, from this point of view, and any other form is to be considered as the "efficient" overstressing of one or another of the ingredients found in ritual drama. An essayistic treatise of scientific cast, for instance, would be viewed as a kind of Hamletic soliloquy, its rhythm slowed down to a snail's pace, or perhaps to an irregular jog, and the dramatic situation of which it is a part usually being left unmentioned.[1]

The reference to Hamlet is especially appropriate, in view of the newer interpretation that has been placed upon Hamlet's quandaries. For more than a hundred years, we had been getting a German translation of Hamlet, a translation in terms of romantic idealism, a translation brought into English by Coleridge, who interpreted Hamlet as an Elizabethan Cole-

[1] The Paget theory of "gesture speech" obviously makes a perfect fit with this perspective by correlating the origins of linguistic action with bodily action and posture.

ridge, the "man of inaction." The newer and juster interpretation, which Maurice Evans has done much to restore for us, largely by the simple expedient of giving us the play uncut, is that of Hamlet as the "scientist," a man anxious to weigh all the objective evidence prior to the act. Among other things, it has been pointed out, there was the "scientific" problem (as so conceived within the beliefs current in Shakespeare's day) of determining whether the ghost was *really* the voice of his father or a satanic deception. And Hamlet, as preparation for his act, employed the stolid Horatio and the ruse of the play-within-a-play as "controls," to make sure that his interpretation of the scene was not fallacious, or as we might say, "subjective." [2]

[2] An exceptionally good instance revealing the ways in which dramatic structure underlies essayistic material may be got by inspection of Max Lerner's article, "Constitution and Court as Symbols" (*The Yale Law Journal*, June, 1937). The essay is divided into four parts, or as we should say, four acts. (In modern playwriting, the four-act form has very often replaced the five-act form of earlier Western drama, the climax coming in the third act, with the aftermath of acts IV and V telescoped into one.)

Act I. "Symbols Possess Men." Here the dramatist acquaints us with the situation in which his tragedy is to be enacted. He describes the ways in which leaders prod people to desired forms of action by manipulating the symbols with which these people think. He then narrows the field to the "Constitution as symbol," and places the Supreme Court as a personalized vessel of the constitutional authority.

Act II. "Constitution into Fetich." The action is now under way. Reviewing American history, the dramatist develops in anecdotal arpeggio the proposition summed up by a timeless level of abstraction in Act I. The act ends on "evidence of the disintegration of the constitutional symbol," a theme that will be carried an important step farther in—

Act III. "Divine Right: American Plan." The Justices of the Supreme Court are here presented as our equivalent for king-ship and godhead. And the act ends on the tragic crime, the symbolic slaying of the sacrificial king, as the author is attacking our "kings" (i.e., he advocates their deposition from authority). In a footnote, the symmetry is rounded out by a kind of "funeral oration" that gives the slain fathers their dues: "There seems to be something about the judicial robes that not only hypnotizes the beholder but transforms the wearer; Marshall and Taney are the principal, but not the only, instances of men whose capacities for greatness no one suspected until they faced the crucial tasks of the Court." Thus, in both their malign and benign functions, these offerings are "worthy" of sacrifice.

Act IV. "New Symbols for Old." The result of the slaying is indeed a

The objection may be raised that "historically" the ritual drama is *not* the Ur-form. If one does not conceive of ritual drama in a restricted sense (but allows for a "broad interpretation" whereby a Greek goat-song and a savage dance to tom-toms in behalf of fertility, rain, or victory could be put in the same bin), a good argument could be adduced, even on the historical, or genetic, interpretation of the Ur-form. However, from my point of view, even if it were proved beyond all question that the ritual drama is not by any means the poetic prototype from which all other forms of poetic and critical expression have successively broken off (as dissociated fragments each made "efficient" within its own rights), my proposal would be in no way impaired. Let ritual drama be proved, for instance, to be the *last* form historically developed; or let it be proved to have arisen anywhere along the line. There would be no embarrassment: we could contend, for instance, that the earlier forms were but groping towards it, as rough drafts, with the ritual drama as the perfection of these trends—while subsequent forms could be treated as "departures" from it, a kind of "esthetic fall."

The reason for our lack of embarrassment is that we are not upholding this perspective on the basis of historical or genetic material. We are proposing it as a *calculus*—a vocabulary, or set of coordinates, that serves best for the integration of all phenomena studied by the *social* sciences. We propose it as the logical alternative to the treatment of human acts and relations in terms of the mechanistic metaphor (stimulus, re-

---

surprise, if approached from other than the dramatic point of view. For a new vision emerges, a vision of the basic motives by which men are moved. And strangely enough, these "transcendent" motives are *hunger* and *fear*. They are *naturalistic* motives. The dramatist, released by the slaying of the fathers, has "gone primitive." The coordinates of the previous acts had been distinctly *social;* and, as anyone acquainted with Lerner's brilliant studies is aware, the coordinates customary to this author are social; but here, for the moment, the symbolic slaying surprises him into a new quality, a "Saturnalian" vision. The episode is, of course, essayistically refurbished elsewhere so that social coordinates are regained. I am here but discussing the form of this one article, taken as an independent integer.

sponse, and the conditioned reflex). And we propose it, along with the contention that mechanistic considerations need not be *excluded* from such a perspective, but take their part in it, as a statement about the predisposing structure of the *ground* or *scene* upon which the drama is enacted.[3]

Are we in an "Augustinian" period or a "Thomistic" one?

[3] In work on which I am now engaged, as a kind of "Prolegomena to any future imputation of motives," I have been applying coordinates that can, I think, carry a step further the ways of locating and distinguishing motivational elements. I now distinguish the three voices, active, passive, and middle (reflexive), as they show motivationally in theories stressing action, passion, and mediation. And instead of the situation-strategy pair, I now use five terms: act, scene, agent, agency, purpose.

These five terms, with a treatment of the purely internal or syntactic relationships prevailing among them, are I think particularly handy for extending the discussion of motivation so as to locate the strategies in metaphysical and theological systems, in accounts of the Creation, in theories of law and constitutionality, and in the shifts between logic and history, being and becoming, as these shifts occur in theories of motivation.

The use of this fuller terminology in the synopsizing of fictional works would require no major emendations in the methods discussed. But I might, as a result of it, be able to state the basic rules of thumb in a more precise way, thus:

The critic is trying to *synopsize* the given work. He is trying to synopsize it, not in the degenerated sense which the word "synopsis" now usually has for us, as meaning a mere "skeleton or outline of the plot or argument," but in the sense of "conveying comprehensively," or "getting at the basis of." And one can work towards this basis, or essence, from without, by "scissor-work" as objective as the nature of the materials permits, in focussing all one's attention about the *motivation,* which is identical with *structure.*

Hence, one will watch, above all, every reference that bears upon expectancy and foreshadowing, in particular every overt reference to any kind of "calling" or "compulsion" (i.e., active or passive concept of motive). And one will note particularly the *situational* or *scenic* material (the "properties") in which such references are contexts; for in this way he will find the astrological relationships prevailing between the plot and the background, hence being able to treat scenic material as representative of psychic material (for instance, if he has distinguished between a motivation in the sign of day and a motivation in the sign of night, as explicitly derivable by citation from the book itself, and if he now sees night falling, he recognizes that the quality of motivation may be changing, with a new kind of act being announced by the change of scene).

"Faith" cannot act relevantly without "knowledge"— "knowledge" cannot act at all without "faith." But though each requires the other, there is a difference of emphasis possible. The great political confusion of the present, which is matched in the poetic sphere by a profusion of rebirth rituals, with a great rise of adolescent characters as the bearers of "representative" roles (adolescence being the transitional stage *par excellence*), gives reason to believe that we are in a kind of "neo-evangelical" era, struggling to announce a new conception of purpose. And we believe that such a state of affairs would require more of the "Augustinian" stress upon the *agon*, the contest, with knowledge as the Hamletic preparation for the act required in this agon. Scientific pragmatism, as seen from this point of view, would be considered less as a philosophical assertion per se than as the lore of the "complicating factors" involved in any philosophic assertion. It would be a *necessary admonitory adjunct* to any philosophy, and thus could and should be engrafted as an essential corrective ingredient in any philosophy; its best service is in admonishing us *what to look out for* in any philosophic assertion.

The relation between the "drama" and the "dialectic" is obvious. Plato's dialectic was appropriately written in the mode of ritual drama. It is concerned with the maieutic, or midwifery, of philosophic assertion, the ways in which an idea is developed by the "cooperative competition" of the "parliamentary." Inimical assertions are invited to collaborate in the perfecting of the assertion. In fact, the greatest menace *to* dictatorships lies in the fact that, through their "efficiency" in silencing the enemy, they deprive themselves of competitive collaboration. Their assertion lacks the opportunity to mature through "agonistic" development. By putting the quietus upon their opponent, they bring themselves all the more rudely against the *unanswerable opponent,* the opponent who cannot be refuted, the nature of brute reality itself. Insofar as their chart of meanings is inadequate as a description of the scene, it is not equipped to encompass the scene. And by silencing the opponent, it deprives itself of the full value to be got from the "collective revelation" to the maturing of which a vocal opposition radically contributes.

And there is a "collective revelation," a social structure of meanings by which the individual forms himself. Recent emphasis upon the great amount of superstition and error in the beliefs of savages has led us into a false emphasis here. We have tended to feel that a whole collectivity can be "wrong" in its chart of meanings. On the contrary, if a chart of meanings were ever "wrong," it would die in one generation. Even the most superstition-ridden tribe must have had many very accurate ways of sizing up real obstacles and opportunities in the world, for otherwise it could not have maintained itself. Charts of meaning are not "right" or "wrong"—they are relative *approximations* to the truth. And only insofar as they contain real ingredients of the truth can the men who hold them perpetuate their progeny. In fact, even in some of the most patently "wrong" charts, there are sometimes discoverable ingredients of "rightness" that have been lost in our perhaps "closer" approximations. A ritual dance for promoting the fertility of crops was absurd enough as "science" (though its absurdity was effectively and realistically corrected insofar as the savage, along with the mummery of the rite, planted the seed; and if you do not abstract the rite as the essence of the event, but instead consider the act of planting as also an important ingredient of the total recipe, you see that the chart of meanings contained a very important accuracy). It should also be noted that the rite, considered as "social science," had an accuracy lacking in much of our contemporary action, since it was highly *collective* in its attributes, a *group dance* in which *all* shared, hence an incantatory device that kept alive a much stronger sense of the group's consubstantiality than is stimulated today by the typical acts of private enterprise.

In equating "dramatic" with "dialectic," we automatically have also our perspective for the analysis of history, which is a "dramatic" process, involving dialectical oppositions. And if we keep this always in mind, we are reminded that every document bequeathed us by history must be treated as a *strategy for encompassing a situation*. Thus, when considering some document like the American Constitution, we shall be automatically warned not to consider it in isolation, but as the *answer* or *rejoinder* to assertions current in the situation in which it arose. We must take this into account when confronting now the problem of abiding by its "principles" in a situation that puts forth questions totally different from those prevailing at the time when the document was formed. We should thus claim as our allies, in embodying the "dramatic perspective," those modern critics who point out that our Constitution is to be considered as a rejoinder to the theories and practices of mercantilist paternalism current at the time of its establishment.[4]

[4] In this connection, we might note a distinction between positive and dialectical terms—the former being terms that do not require an opposite to define them, the latter being terms that do require an opposite. "Apple," for instance, is a positive term, in that we do not require, to understand it, the concept of a "counter-apple." But a term like "freedom" is dialectical, in that we cannot locate its meaning without reference to some concept of enslavement, confinement, or restriction. And "capitalism" is not a positive term, but a dialectical one to be defined by reference to the concepts of either "feudalism" or "socialism."

Our courts consider the Constitution in accordance with theories of positive law—yet actually the Constitution is a dialectical instrument; and one cannot properly interpret the course of judicial decisions unless he treats our "guaranties of constitutional rights" not as positive terms but as dialectical ones.

Our Bill of Rights, for instance, is composed of clauses that descended from two substantially different situations. First, as emerging in Magna Carta, they were enunciated by the feudal barons in their "reactionary" struggles against the "progressive" rise of central authority. Later, in the British Petition of Right and Bill of Rights, they were enunciated by the merchant class in their "progressive" struggles against the "reactionary" resistance of the Crown. It is in this second form that they came into our Constitution.

BUT:

Note this important distinction: in the British Bill of Rights, they were defined, or located, as a resistance of the *people* to the *Crown*. Thus they had, at this stage, a strongly collectivistic quality, as the people were united in a common cause against the Crown, and the rights were thus dialectically defined with relation to this opposition. The position of the Crown, in other words, was a necessary term in giving meaning to the people's counterassertions.

Where does the drama get its materials? From the "unending conversation" that is going on at the point in history when we are born. Imagine that you enter a parlor. You come late. When you arrive, others have long preceded you, and they are engaged in a heated discussion, a discussion too heated for them to pause and tell you exactly what it is about. In fact,

---

In the United States document, however, the Crown had been abolished. Hence, the dialectical function of the Crown in giving meaning to the terms would have to be taken over by some other concept of sovereignty. And the only sovereign within the realm covered by the Constitution was the *government elected by the people*. Hence, since the opposite "cooperates" in the definition of a dialectical term, and since the sovereignty or authority against which the rights were proclaimed had changed from that of an antipopular Crown to that of a popularly representative government, it would follow that the quality of the "rights" themselves would have to change. And such change of quality did take place, in that the rights became interpreted as rights of the people as *individuals* or *minorities* against a government representing the will of the people as a *collectivity* or *majority*.

Eventually, this interpretation assisted the rise of the great supercorporations, linked by financial ties and interlocking directorates. And these supercorporations gradually come to be considered as a new seat of authority, placed outside the direct control of parliamentary election. And as this kind of business sovereignty becomes recognized as *bona fide* sovereignty, you begin to see a new change taking place in the "dialectical" concept of constitutional rights. For theorists begin now to think of these rights as assertions against the encroachments of the supercorporations (the New Crown). That is: the tendency is to think once more of the rights as claimed by the people as a *majority* against the rule of the supercorporations as a sovereign minority.

However, the statement that a term is "dialectical," in that it derives its meaning from an opposite term, and that the opposite term may be different at different historical periods, does not at all imply that such terms are "meaningless." All we need do is to decide what they are *against* at a given period (in brief, to recognize that the Constitution cannot be interpreted as a positive document, but must continually be treated as an *act in a scene outside it,* hence to recognize that we must always consider "the Constitution *beneath* the Constitution," or "the Constitution *above* the Constitution," or "the Constitution *beyond* the Constitution," which may as you prefer be higher law, divine law, the laws of biology, or of big business, or of little business, etc.). Much of the cruder linguistic analysis done by the debunko-semanticist school involves the simple fallacy of failing to note the distinction between positive and dialectical terms, whereby, in applying to *dialectical* terms the instruments of analysis proper to *positive* terms, they can persuade themselves that the terms are meaningless.

the discussion had already begun long before any of them got there, so that no one present is qualified to retrace for you all the steps that had gone before. You listen for a while, until you decide that you have caught the tenor of the argument; then you put in your oar. Someone answers; you answer him; another comes to your defense; another aligns himself against you, to either the embarrassment or gratification of your opponent, depending upon the quality of your ally's assistance. However, the discussion is interminable. The hour grows late, you must depart. And you do depart, with the discussion still vigorously in progress.

It is from this "unending conversation" (the vision at the basis of Mead's work) that the materials of your drama arise.[5] Nor is this verbal action all there is to it. For all these words are grounded in what Malinowski would call "contexts of situation." And very important among these "contexts of situation" are the kind of factors considered by Bentham, Marx, and Veblen, the material interests (of private or class structure) that you symbolically defend or symbolically appropriate or symbolically align yourself with in the course of making your own assertions. These interests do not "cause" your discussion; its "cause" is in the genius of man himself as *homo loquax*. But they greatly affect the *idiom* in which you speak, and so the idiom by which you think. Or, if you would situate the genius of man in a *moral* aptitude, we could say that this moral aptitude is universally present in all men, to varying degrees, but that it must express itself through a medium, and this medium is in turn grounded in material structures. In different property structures, the moral aptitude has a correspondingly different idiom through which to speak.

By the incorporation of these social idioms we build our-

[5] Also, it is in this "unending conversation" that the assertions of any given philosopher are grounded. *Strategically*, he may present his work as departing from some "rock-bottom fact" (he starts, for instance: "I look at this table. I perceive it to have. . . ." etc.). Actually, the very selection of his "rock-bottom fact" derives its true grounding from the current state of the conversation, and assumes quite a different place in the "hierarchy of facts" when the locus of discussion has shifted.

selves, our "personalities," i.e., our *roles* (which brings us
again back into the matter of the drama). The movie version
of Shaw's *Pygmalion* shows us the process in an almost terri-
fyingly simplified form, as we observe his heroine building
herself a character synthetically, by mastering the insignia, the
linguistic and manneristic labels of the class among whom she
would, by this accomplishment, symbolically enroll herself
(with the promise that this symbolic enrollment would culmi-
nate in objective, material fulfillment). In its simplicity, the
play comes close to heresy, as might be revealed by matching
it with a counterheresy: Joyce's individualistic, absolutist, "dic-
tatorial" establishment of a language from within. Shaw's
heroine, in making herself over by artificially acquiring an
etiquette of speech and manners, is "internalizing the external"
(the term is Mead's). But Joyce is "externalizing the internal."

I call both of these "heresies" because I do not take a heresy
to be a flat opposition to an orthodoxy (except as so made to
appear under the "dialectical pressure" arising from the fact
that the two philosophies may become insignia of opposed
material forces); I take a heresy rather to be the isolation of
one strand in an orthodoxy, and its following-through-with-
rational-efficiency to the point where "logical conclusion" cannot be distinguished from *"reductio ad absurdum."* An
"orthodox" statement here would require us to consider complementary movements: both an internalizing of the external
and an externalizing of the internal. Heresies tend to present
themselves as arguments rather than as dictionaries. An argument must ideally be consistent, and tactically must at least
have the *appearance* of consistency. But a dictionary need not
aim at consistency: it can quite comfortably locate a mean by
terms signalizing contradictory extremes.[6]

[6] An ideal philosophy, from this point of view, would seek to satisfy
the requirements of a perfect dictionary. It would be a calculus
(matured by constant reference to the "collective revelation" that
is got by a social *body* of thought) for charting the nature of events
and for clarifying all important relationships. In practice, however, a
philosophy is developed partially *in opposition to other philosophies,*
so that tactics of refutation are involved, thus tending to give the

The broad outlines of our position might be codified thus:

(1) We have the drama and the scene of the drama. The drama is enacted against a background.

(2) The description of the scene is the role of the physical

---

philosopher's calculus the stylistic form of a lawyer's plea.

The connection between philosophy and law (moral and political) likewise contributes to the "lawyer's brief" strategy of presentation. The philosopher thus is often led to attempt "proving" his philosophy by proving its "justice" in the abstract, whereas the only "proof" of a philosophy, considered as a calculus, resides in showing, by concrete application, the scope, complexity, and accuracy of its coordinates for charting the nature of events. Thus, the name for "house" would not be primarily tested for "consistency" with the names for "tree" or "money." One would reveal the value of the names by revealing their correspondence with some important thing, function, or relationship. This is what we mean by saying that a philosophy, as a "chart," is quite at home in contradictions.

I recall a man, for instance, of "heretical" cast, who came to me with a sorrow of this sort: "How can you ever have a belief in human rationality," he complained, "when you see things like this?" And he showed me a news clipping about a truck driver who had received a prize for driving his truck the maximum distance without an accident. When asked how he did it, the truck driver answered: "I had two rules: Give as much of the road as you can, and take as much as you can." I saw in this no grounds to despair of human reason; on the contrary, I thought that the prize winner had been a very moral truck driver, and I was glad to read that, for once at least, such great virtue had been rewarded. This was true Aristotelian truck driving, if I ever saw it; and whatever else one may say against Aristotle, I never heard him called "irrational."

What, in fact, is "rationality" but the desire for an *accurate chart for naming what is going on?* Isn't this what Spinoza had in mind, when calling for a philosophy whose structure would parallel the structure of reality? We thus need not despair of human rationality, even in eruptive days like ours. I am sure that even the most arbitrary of Nazis can be shown to possess it; for no matter how inadequate his chart of meaning may be as developed under the deprivations of the quietus and oversimplifying dialectical pressure, he at least *wants* it to tell him accurately *what is going on* in his world and in the world at large.

Spinoza perfected an especially inventive strategy, by this stress upon the "adequate idea" as the ideal of a chart, for uniting free will and determinism, with rationality as the bridge. For if one's meanings are correct, he will choose the wiser of courses; in this he will be "rational"; as a rational man, he will "want" to choose this wiser course; and as a rational man he will "*have* to want" to choose this wiser course.

sciences; the description of the drama is the role of the social sciences.

(3) The physical sciences are a calculus of events; the social sciences are a calculus of acts. And human affairs being dramatic, the discussion of human affairs becomes dramatic criticism, with more to be learned from a study of tropes than from a study of tropisms.

(4) Criticism, in accordance with its methodological ideal, should attempt to develop rules of thumb that can be adopted and adapted (thereby giving it the maximum possibility of development via the "collective revelation," a development from first approximation to closer approximation, as against the tendency, particularly in impressionistic criticism and its many scientific variants that do not go by this name, to be forever "starting from scratch").

(5) The error of the social sciences has usually resided in the attempt to appropriate the scenic calculus for a charting of the act.

(6) However, there is an interaction between scene and role. Hence, dramatic criticism takes us into areas that involve the act as "response" to the scene. Also, although there may theoretically be a common scenic background for all men when considered as a collectivity, the acts of other persons become part of the scenic background for any individual person's act.

(7) Dramatic criticism, in the idiom of theology, considered the individual's act with relation to God as a personal background. Pantheism proclaimed the impersonality of this divine role. I.e., whereas theology treated the scenic function of Nature as a "representative" of God, pantheism made the natural background identical with God. It narrowed the circumference of the context in which the act would be located. Naturalism pure and simple sought to eliminate the role of divine participation completely, though often with theological vestiges, as with the "God-function" implicit in the idea of "progressive evolution," where God now took on a "historicist" role. History, however, deals with "events," hence the increas-

ing tendency in the social sciences to turn from a calculus of the act to a "pure" calculus of the event. Hence, in the end, the ideal of stimulus-response psychology.

(8) Whatever may be the character of existence in the physical realm, this realm functions but as scenic background when considered from the standpoint of the human realm. I.e., it functions as "lifeless," as mere "property" for the drama. And an ideal calculus for charting this physical realm must treat it as lifeless (in the idiom of mechanistic determinism). But to adopt such a calculus for the charting of life is to chart by a "planned incongruity" (i.e., a treatment of something in terms of what it is *not*).

(9) The ideal calculus of dramatic criticism would require, not an incongruity, but an inconsistency. I.e., it would be required to employ the coordinates of *both* determinism *and* free will.

(10) Since, like biology, it is in a realm midway between vital assertions and lifeless properties, the realm of the dramatic (hence of dramatic criticism) is neither physicalist nor antiphysicalist, but physicalist-plus.

Narrowing our discussion from consideration of the social drama in general to matters of poetry in particular, we may note that the distinction between the "internalizing of the external" and the "externalizing of the internal" involves two different functions of imagery: imagery as confessional and imagery as incantatory, the two elements that John Crowe Ransom has isolated from Aristotle's *Poetics* in his chapters on "The Cathartic Principle" and "The Mimetic Principle." Imagery, as confessional, contains in itself a kind of "personal irresponsibility," as we may even relieve ourselves of private burdens by befouling the public medium. If our unburdening attains an audience, it has been "socialized" by the act of reception. In its public reception, even the most "excremental" of poetry becomes "exonerated" (hence the extreme anguish of a poet who, writing "with maximum efficiency" under such an esthetic, does not attain absolution by the suffrage of customers).

But we must consider also the "incantatory" factor in imagery: its function as a device for inviting us to "make ourselves over in the image of the imagery." Seen from this point of view, a thoroughly "confessional" art may enact a kind of "individual salvation at the expense of the group." Quite as the development of the "enlightenment" in the economic sphere was from a collective to an individual emphasis (with "private enterprise" as the benign phase of an attitude which has its malign counterpart in the philosophy of "*sauve qui peut*— and the devil take the hindmost"), so have mass rituals tended to be replaced by individualist revisions, with many discriminations that adjust them with special accuracy to the particular needs of their inventor and "signer"; while this mode in turn attains its logical conclusion or reduction to absurdity in poetry having the maximum degree of confessional efficiency, a kind of literary metabolistic process that may satisfy the vital needs of the poet well enough, but through poetic passages that leave offal in their train. Such puns seem to have been consciously exploited by Joyce when he is discussing his *ars poetica* in *Finnegans Wake*, hence should be considered by any reader looking for the work's motivations (i.e., the center about which its structure revolves, or the law of its development). Freud's "cloacal theory" would offer the simplest explanation as to the ways in which the sexually private and the excrementally private may become psychologically merged, so that this theme could be treated as consubstantial with the theme of incest previously mentioned.

For if we test the efficient confessional (as perhaps best revealed in a writer like Faulkner) from the standpoint of the incantatory (from the standpoint of its exhortation to "come on" and make ourselves over in the image of its imagery), we quickly realize its sinister function, from the standpoint of over-all social necessities. By the "incantatory" test, a sadistic poetry, when reinforced by the imaginative resources of genius, seems to be a perfect match, in the esthetic sphere, to the "incantatory" nature of our mounting armament in the practical or political sphere, or to the efficiency of newspaper headlines (got by the formation and training of worldwide organizations devoted to the culling of conflicts, calamities, cataclysms, and atrocities "rationally" selected from the length and breadth of all human society, and given as our "true" representation of that day's "reality").

Confessional efficiency, in its range from poem to report, has given rise to an equally fallacious counterefficiency which, recognizing the incantatory function of imagery, diligently selects for "reassuring" purposes. Hence, the confessional emphasis of the nineteenth century was "dialectically complemented" by an esthetic of easy optimism, merging into the sentimental and hypocritical, making peace with the disasters in the world by flatly decreeing that "all's right with the world." I think that much of Whitman's appeal resides in this poetic alchemy, whereby the dangerous destruction of our natural resources could be exaltedly interpreted as an "advance"—while simple doctrines of automatic and inevitable progressive evolution were its replica in the "scientific" bin.

So, in sum, we had two opposite excesses: the "cathartic" poetry which would relieve the poet of his spell by transferring its malignities to his audience, insofar as he was capable of doing so (as the Ancient Mariner got a measure of relief from his curse by a magnetic transference from himself to the wedding-guest, and by the disasters besetting the Pilot's boy). It is an art that tries to "leave the spell upon us," an art that I would propose to sum up as the "esthetic of the Poe story," a "monotonic" art, from which the reader can escape only by refusal, by being "wholesomely trivial" enough to respond but superficially to the poet's incantations. And we had a "mimetic" poetry that did proceed on the recognition of the incantatory quality in imagery (its function in inviting us to assume the attitudes corresponding to its gestures), but was disposed towards the strategy of the "idealistic lie," in simply renaming an evil as a good, establishing solace by magical decree.

Perhaps the situation is most clearly revealed in music, in the gradual change from "symphony" to "tone poem," with Liszt as an important fulcrum in the change. The symphonic form contained a "way in," "way through," and "way out." It sought to place a spell of danger upon us, and in the assertion of its *finale* to release us from this spell. But the tone poem sought *to lead us in and leave us there*, to have us sink beneath the ground with Alpheus and never to reemerge with Arethusa. It sought to *bewitch* us—and our only protection against it was either triviality of response or infection by a hundred other witcheries, a general clutter of spells, so falling across one another on the bias, that in their confusion they somewhat neutralized the effects of one another.

As regards the borderline area, in which the symbolic act of art overlaps upon the symbolic act in life, I would now offer an anecdote illustrative of spells, and how one might serve the ends of freedom, not by the attempt to eliminate spells (which I consider impossible) but by a critical attempt to coach "good" spells:

A man is, let us say, subject to spells of alcoholic debauchery. For weeks he subsists, in a drugged stupor. After which he recovers, is "purified," and for varying lengths of time rigorously abstains from alcohol.

He also has a sporadic gift for writing. But he cannot sustain this happier kind of spell, and when he relapses into an alcoholic debauch, he has no greater powers of articulacy than a cabbage. His friends say that his weakness for alcohol is gradually destroying his gift for writing; and he also fears this to be the case. Their interpretation seems borne out by a correlation between the two kinds of spell, the malign "gift for" alcoholism and the benign "relapses into" writing. For after he has ended a debauch, and has abstained from alcohol for a time, his literary aptness returns.

He is especially apt, let us say, in depicting the current scene by a felicitous twist of humor that gets things picturesquely awry. And when the benign spell is upon him, some very appealing squibs of this sort occur to him. Then he is happy—and his friends begin to renew their hopes for him. They bestir themselves to assist him in getting the items published.

But what if the correlation between the malign alcoholic spell and the benign literary spell should be differently interpreted? What if they are but different stages along the same graded series, different parts of the same spectrum?

The literary gift of felicitous distortion would thus be but an incipient manifestation of the extreme distortions got by alcohol. Hence, when our hero writes his squibs in the belief that they are the *opposite* of his alcoholism, he may really be turning to the kind of incantation that acts as the "way in" to his period of debauch. Precisely when he thinks he is on the road to recovery, he would have begun the first stage of yielding.

The squibs, that is, are in his psychic economy a representative of the alcohol; they are part of the same cluster; they function synedochically, and thus contain implicitly, as "foreshadowing," the whole of the cluster. Hence, in writing them, he is taking alcohol vicariously. This is not to say that the squibs are a mere "sublimation" of alcoholism; you could with more justice say that the alcoholism is a more "efficient" embodiment of the esthetic exemplified in the squibs. What is got by materialistic manipulation through the taking of the alcohol, *"ex opere operato,"* is but the attainment, in a simplified, restricted idiom, of the effects got in a more complex idiom through the writing of the squibs.

The Latin formula is borrowed from theological controversy about the nature of the sacrament. In pagan magic, the material operations of the sacrament were deemed enough to produce the purification. Ritual purification was a "scientific" process, with the purifying effects got simply by the *material operations* of the rite. No matter of conscience was involved; no private "belief" was thought necessary to the success of the rite. The purification was, rather, thought to operate like the cures of modern medicine (from the mere performing of the correct material acts themselves)—as the effects of castor oil are the same with "believer" and "nonbeliever" alike. Theological tacticians had the problem of taking over the "scientific" magic of paganism and introducing a religious emphasis upon the need of conscience or belief as a factor in the effectiveness of the rite, without thereby implying that the rite was purely "symbolic." The magical doctrine was "realistic"; and similarly, the religious sacrament was "realistic" (that is, the rite was held *really* to have transubstantiated the holy wafers and the wine into the body and blood of Christ: the act was not deemed merely "symbolical," except among schismatics; it was as materialistic a means of purification as castor oil, yet at the same time its effective operation required the collaboration of belief, as castor oil does not; the effect could not be got, as with pagan magic and scientific materialism, through the objective operation alone, i.e., *ex opere operato*). We find this delicate state of indeterminacy in the relation between the squibs and the alcoholism, though the "piety" here is of a sort different from that considered as the norm by orthodox Christian theologians: a piety more in keeping perhaps with the genius of Bacchantic services, the cult of methodic distortion that stressed the element of Priapic obscenities and finally became sophisticated, alembicated, and attenuated in comedy. The writing of the squibs corresponds to the stage aimed at by the theologians: it is a material operation, yet at the same time it requires "belief." The alcoholic stage is purely materialistic, the results now being attained efficiently by the "real" power of the substance alone.

But note the ironic element here. If the writing of the squibs is in the same equational structure with the taking of the alcohol, in writing the squibs it is as though our hero had "taken his first drink." This is the one thing he knows he must not do. For he knows that he is incapable of moderation, once the first drink has been taken. But if the squibs and the alcohol are in the same cluster, he has vicariously taken the first drink in the very act which, on its social face, was thought by him and his friends to belong in an opposing cluster.

Thus, he has begun his "way in." He has begun infecting himself with a kind of incantation that synedochically foreshadows, or implicitly contains, the progression from this less efficient, ritualistic yielding to an efficient, practical yielding: he has begun the chain of developments that finally leads into alcohol as the most direct means of embodying the same esthetic of distortion as was embodied in his squibs.

The irony is that, if he wanted to guard properly against relapse, *instead of writing the squibs, he would resolutely refuse to write them.* He would recognize that, however it may be in the case of other men, in his case he conjures forth a djinn(or, if you will, gin) that will come at his beckoning but will develop powers of its own, once summoned. He may know the magical incantations that summon it; but he does not know the magical incantations that compel it to obey him, once it has been summoned; hence, let him not summon it.

Would this mean that our hero should not write at all? I do not think so. On the contrary, I think it means that he should *attempt to coach some other kind of writing, of a different incantatory quality.* From this kind he would rigorously exclude the slightest distortion, no matter how appealing such distortion might be. *For him,* such distortions are in the category of intemperance, regardless of what category they may be in *for others.* Only thus, by deliberately refusing to cultivate such incantatory modes, would he be avoiding a "way in" to a dangerous state of mind and utilizing a mode of incantation truly oppositional to his weakness.[7]

We are not proposing here a mere literary variant of Buchmanism. We take it for granted that our hero's alcoholism is also interwoven with a material context of situation, which

[7] I should contend that our hero, in thus altering his incantatory methods, would get greater freedom by acting more rationally. Others, however, might consider any incantation as per se a sign of "irrationality." The issue probably resolves into two contrasting theories of consciousness. There is a one-way theory, which holds that freedom is got by a kind of drainage, drawing something ("energy"?) from the unconscious and irrational into the conscious and rational. I call this the "reservoir theory," according to which a "dark" reservoir is tapped and its contents are gradually pumped into a "light" reservoir, the quantities being in inverse proportion to each other. Against this, I should propose a two-way, "dialectical" theory, with "conscious" and "unconscious" considered as reciprocal functions of each other, growing or diminishing concomitantly. An infant, by this theory, would be sparse in "unconscious" (with sparse dreams) owing to the sparsity of its consciousness (that provides the material for dreams). And by this theory, the attempt to "drain off" the unconscious would be absurd. Instead, one should seek to "harness" it. I believe that this dialectical theory, as ultimately developed, would require that *charitas,* rather than "intelligence," be considered as the primary faculty of adjustment.

has become similarly endowed with "incantatory" quality, and must be critically inspected from the standpoint of the possibility that many environmental ingredients would also require alteration. We do hold, however, that environmental factors which one is personally unable to change can be given a different incantatory quality by a change of one's relationship towards them (as with a change of allegiance from one band to another).

It is, then, my contention, that if we approach poetry from the standpoint of situations and strategies, we can make the most relevant observations about both the content and the form of poems. By starting from a concern with the various tactics and deployments involved in ritualistic acts of membership, purification, and opposition, we can most accurately discover "what is going on" in poetry. I contend that the "dramatic perspective" is the unifying hub for this approach. And that it is not to be "refuted," as a calculus, by introducing some "argument" from logic or genetics, or simply by listing a host of other possible perspectives; the only serviceable argument for another calculus would be its explicit proclamation and the illustrating of its scope by concrete application. I do not by any means maintain that no other or better calculus is possible. I merely maintain that the advocate of an alternative calculus should establish its merits, not in the abstract, but by "filling it out," by showing, through concrete applications to poetic materials, its scope and relevance.

Some students, however, seem to feel that this perspective vows us to a neglect of the "realistic" element in poetry. Its stress upon processes of ritual and stylization, they feel, too greatly implies that the poet is making passes in the air, mere blandishments that look silly, as tested by the "realistic" criteria of science.

In the first place, I would recall my distinction between "realism" and "naturalism," as a way of suggesting that much we call "realism" in science should be more accurately called "naturalism." In the esthetic field, "naturalism" is a mode of "debunking." Where some group ideal is being exploited for malign purposes (as when the scoundrel has recourse to patriotism in cloaking his unpatriotic acts), the "naturalist" will proceed "efficiently" by debunking not only the scoundrel but the patriotism. Or he will "debunk" the religious hypocrite by "debunking" religion itself. Thurman Arnold's "scientific" analysis of social relations in his *Folklore of Capitalism* is largely of this "naturalistic" cast, leading him finally to a flat dissociation between the "scientist" and the "citizen." To act as a "citizen," by his criteria, one must participate in certain forms of political mummery. But to diagnose as a "scientist," one should simply "expose" this mummery.

Now, I grant that there is much faulty mummery in the world. But where a structure of analysis is found to vow one to a flat antithesis between one's role as scientist and one's role as citizen, we should at least consider the possibility that the structure of analysis itself may be at fault. And I think that the distinction between the strategies of "realism" and "naturalism" may provide us with a handy way in to this matter.

Scientific "naturalism" is a lineal descendant of nominalism, a school that emerged in the late Middle Ages as an opponent of scholastic realism. And we might sum up the distinction between realism and nominalism, from the standpoint of strategies, by saying that *realism considered individuals as members of a group, whereas nominalism considered groups as aggregates of individuals.* We thus observe that the nominalist controversy, finally incorporated in the Franciscan order, prepared for scientific skepticism in undermining the group coordinates upon which church thought was founded, and also prepared for the individualistic emphasis of private enterprise.

This individualistic emphasis led in turn to naturalism. Thus, I should call Dos Passos a naturalist rather than a realist. And I should call the "hard-boiled" style today a kind of "academic school of naturalism" (a characterization suggesting that Steinbeck's sociality is still encumbered by "nonrealistic" vestiges). As used by Arnold, the naturalist-nominalist perspective finally leads to the assumption that the devices employed in a *group* act are mere "illusions," and that the "scientific truth" about human relations is discovered from an individualistic point of view, from outside the requirements of group action. One reviewer, intending to praise his book, hit upon the most damning line of all, in calling it a "challenge to right, center, and left," which is pretty much the same as saying that it is a "challenge" to *any* kind of social action.

But let us try out a hypothetical case. Suppose that some disaster has taken place, and that I am to break the information to a man who will suffer from the knowledge of it. The disaster is a *fact,* and I am going to *communicate this fact.* Must I not still make a *choice of stylization* in the communication of this fact? I may communicate it "gently" or "harshly," for instance. I may try to "protect" the man somewhat from the suddenness of the blow; or I may so "strategize" my information that I reinforce the blow. Indeed, it may even be that the information is as much a blow to me as it is to him, and that I may obtain for myself a certain measure of relief from my own discomfiture by "collaborating with the information": I may so phrase it that I take out some of my own suffering from the information by using it dramatically as an instrument for striking him. Or I may offer a somewhat similar outlet for both of us, by also showing that a certain person "is to blame" for the disaster, so that we can convert some of our unhappiness into anger, with corresponding relief to ourselves.

Now, note that in every one of these cases I have communicated "the fact." Yet note also that there are many different *styles* in which I can communicate this "fact." The question of "realistic accuracy" is not involved; for in every case, after I have finished, the auditor knows that the particular disaster, about which I had to inform him, has taken place. I have simply made a choice among possible styles—*and I could not avoid such a choice.* There is no "unstylized" feature here except the disastrous event itself (and even that may have a "stylistic" ingredient, in that it might be felt as more of a blow if coming at a certain time than if it had come at a certain other time—a "stylistic" matter of timing that I, as the imparter of the information, may parallel, in looking for the best or worst moment at which to impart my information).

I should call it a "naturalistic" strategy of communication if I so stylized the informative act as to accept the minimum of "group responsibility" in my choice. If I communicated the fact, for instance, without sympathy for the auditor. Or even more so, if I did have sympathy for the auditor, and the fact was as disastrous to me as it was to him, but I "took it out on" him by reinforcing the blow rather than softening it. And I should call it a "realistic" strategy if I stylized my statement with the maximum sympathy (or "group attitude").

Do not get me wrong. I am not by any means absolutely equating "science" with "naturalism." I am saying that there is a so-called science that identifies "truth" with "debunking"— and I am simply trying to point out that *such "truth" is no less a "stylization" than any other.* The man who embodies it in his work may be as "tender-minded" as the next fellow; usually, in fact, I think that he is even more so—as will be revealed when you find his "hard hitting" at one point in his communication compensated by a great humanitarian softness at another point (which, as I have tried to show elsewhere, is patly the case with Arnold).

Stylization is inevitable. Sometimes it is done by sentimentalization (saying "It's all right" when it isn't). Sometimes by the reverse, brutalization, saying it with an over-bluntness, in "hard-boiled" or its "scientific" equivalents (sadism if you like to write it, masochism if you like to read it). I recall a surrealistic movie that revealed the kind of "protection" we may derive from this strategy, in the esthetic field where the information to be imparted is usually not quite so "disastrous" as the hypothetical event we have been just considering. The movie opens with a view of a man sharpening his razor. We next see a close-up of his eye, an enormous eye filling the entire screen. And then, slowly and systematically, the blade of the razor is drawn across this eye, and in horror we observe it splitting open. Many other horrors follow, but we have been "immunized" by the first shock. We are calloused; we have already been through the worst; there is nothing else to fear; as regards further pain, we have become *roués*. Sometimes the stylization is by neutral description, the method more normal to scientific procedure. And tragedy uses the stylization of ennoblement, making the calamity bearable by making the calamitous situation dignified.

From this point of view we could compare and contrast strategies of motivation in Bentham, Coleridge, Marx, and Mannheim. Bentham, as "debunker," discusses motives "from the bottom up." That is: they are treated as "eulogistic coverings" for "material interests." Coleridge's motivation is "tragic," or "dignifying," "from the top down" (in his phrasing: "*a Jove principium*"). He treats material interests as a limited aspect of "higher" interests. Marx employs a factional strategy of motivation, in debunking the motives of the bourgeois enemy and dignifying the motives of the proletarian ally. Since he has reversed the values of idealism, he would not consider the material grounding of proletarian interests as an indignity. The proletarian view is dignified by being equated with truth, in contrast with the "idealistic lie" of a class that has special prerogatives to protect by systematic misstatements about the nature of reality. Mannheim seeks to obtain a kind of "documentary" perspective on the subject of motives, on a "second level" of generalization. That is: he accepts not only the Marxist debunking of bourgeois motives, but also the bourgeois counterdebunking of proletarian motives; and he next proceeds to attenuate the notion of "debunking" ("unmasking") into a more neutral concept that we might in English call "discounting" or "making allowance for."

Or let us consider another hypothetical case. A man would enroll himself in a cause. His choice may be justified on thoroughly "realistic" grounds. He surveys the situation, sizes it up accurately, decides that a certain strategy of action is required to encompass it and that a certain group or faction is organized to carry out this strategy. Nothing could be more "realistic." Yet suppose that he would write a poem in which, deliberately or spontaneously, he would "stylize" the processes of identification involved in this choice. His act, no matter how thoroughly attuned to the requirements of his times, will be a "symbolic act," hence open to the kind of analysis we have proposed for the description of a symbolic act. If his choice of faction is relevant to the needs of the day, its "realism" is obvious. If the chart of meanings into which he fits this choice of faction are adequate, the relevance is obvious. And to call his poetic gestures merely "illusory" would be like calling it "illusory" when a man, wounded, "stylizes" his response by either groaning or gritting his teeth and flexing his muscles.

There is, in science, a tendency to substitute for ritual, routine. To this extent, there is an antipoetic ingredient in science. It is "poetic" to develop method; it is "scientific" to develop methodology. (From this standpoint, the ideal of literary criticism is a "scientific" ideal.) But we can deceive ourselves if we erect this difference in aim into a distinction between "reality" and "illusion," maintaining that, as judged by the ideals of scientific routine or methodology, the ideals of poetic method, or ritual, become "illusions."

The body is an actor; as an actor, it participates in the movements of the mind, posturing correspondingly; in styles of thought and expression we embody these correlations—and the recognition of this is, as you prefer, either "scientific" or "poetic."

It will thus be seen that, in playing the game of life, we have at our command a resource whereby we can shift the rules of this game. It is as though someone who had been losing at checkers were of a sudden to decide that he had really been playing "give away" (the kind of checkers where the object is not to take as many of your opponent's men as possible, but to lose as many of your own as possible). Where our resources permit, we may piously encourage the awesome, and in so encompassing it, make ourselves immune (by "tolerance," as the word is used of drugs, by Mithridatism). Where our resources do not permit, where we cannot meet such exacting obligations, we may rebel, developing the stylistic antidote that would cancel out an overburdensome awe. And in between these extremes, there is the wide range of the mean, the many instances in which we dilute, attenuate, mixing the ingredient of danger into a recipe of other, more neutral ingredients, wide in their scope and complexity, a chart that concerns itself with the world in all its miraculous diverse plenitude. And for this plenitude of the Creation, being very grateful.

But our symbolic acts can vary greatly in relevance and scope. If we enact by tragedy a purificatory ritual symbolizing our enrollment in a cause shaped to handle a situation accurately, for instance, we may embody the same processes as if we enacted a purificatory ritual symbolizing our enrollment in a cause woefully inadequate to the situation. And the analyst of the two tragedies may, by reason of his over-all classificatory terms, find much in common between the two symbolic acts. The fact remains, however, that one of these acts embodies a chart of meanings superior to the other (and if the chart is too far out of accord with the nature of the situation, the "unanswerable opponent," the objective recalcitrance of the situation itself, will put forth its irrefutable rejoinder).

From *The Philosophy of Literary Form: Studies in Symbolic Action* (2nd ed.; New York: Vintage Books, 1957), pp. 87-113.

Fact, Inference, and Proof in the Analysis
of Literary Symbolism
(1954)

This essay is part of a project called "Theory of the Index,"
concerned with the taking of preparatory notes for purposes of
critical analysis. The hope is to make the analysis of literary
symbolism as systematic as possible, while allowing for an
experimental range required by the subtle and complex nature
of the subject matter.

Fundamentally, the essay is built about the "principle of the
concordance." But whereas concordances, listing all passages
where a given word appears in a text, have been compiled for
a few major works, obviously criticism cannot have the
advantage of such scholarship when studying the terminology
of most literary texts. And even where concordances are
available, there must be grounds for paying more attention to
some terms than to others.

Here, treating the individual words of a work as the basic
"facts" of that work, and using for test case some problems in
the "indexing" of James Joyce's *A Portrait of the Artist as a
Young Man*,[1] the essay asks how to operate with these "facts,"
how to use them as a means of keeping one's inferences under
control, yet how to go beyond them, for purposes of inference,
when seeking to characterize the motives and "salient traits"
of the work, in its nature as a total symbolic structure.

I

Insofar as possible, we confine the realm of the "factual" to a
low but necessary and unquestioned order of observations.

---

[1] For purposes of ready reference, where illustration seems necessary,
the rules and principles discussed here will be illustrated by reference
to a single text, James Joyce's *A Portriat of the Artist as a Young Man.*

Thus, it is a "fact" that the book proper begins, "Once upon a time and a very good time it was . . ." etc., and ends: "Old father, old artificer, stand me now and ever in good stead." We say it is a fact that the "book proper" so begins and so ends. But it is also a "fact" that the text begins with a prior quotation from Ovid's *Metamorphoses* and ends on a reference to duality of scene: "Dublin, 1904/Trieste, 1914." We might get different results, depending upon which of these "facts" we worked from. But in either case, the existence of such "facts" is literally verifiable. "Facts" are what was said or done, as interpreted in the strictest possible sense.

The ideal "atomic fact" in literary symbolism is probably the individual word. We do not say that the literary work is "nothing but" words. We do say that it is "at least" words. True, a word is further reducible to smaller oral and visual particles (letters and phonemes); and such reducibility allows for special cases of "alchemic" transformation whereby the accident of a word's structure may surreptitiously relate it (punwise) to other words that happen to be similar in structure though "semantically" quite distinct from it. But the word is the first full "perfection" of a term. And we move from it either way as our base, either "back" to the dissolution of meaning that threatens it by reason of its accidental punwise associates, or "forward" to its dissolution through inclusion in a "higher meaning," which attains *its* perfection in the sentence.

Surprisingly enough, such a terministic approach to symbolism can be much more "factual" than is the case with reports about actual conditions or happenings in the extra-symbolic realm. In the extrasymbolic realm, there is usually a higher necessary percentage of "interpretation" or "inference" in a statement we call "factual." We can but infer what the diplomat did. But we can cite "factually" some report that says

---

The essay stresses methodological considerations that the critic encounters in attempting to characterize the "salient traits" of this work, in its nature as a symbolic structure. Page numbers refer to the cheapest edition (the Signet paper edition); it is chosen because such indexing usually requires that the book be defaced by indicative markings.

what he did. People usually think that the nonsymbolic realm is the clear one, while the symbolic realm is hazy. But if you agree that the words, or terms, in a book are its "facts," then by the same token you see there is a sense in which we get our view of *deeds* as facts from our sense of *words* as facts, rather than *vice versa*.

In this strict usage, many observations that might ordinarily be treated under the headings of "fact" fall on the side of "inference." For instance, when referring to the formula, "Dublin, 1904/Trieste, 1914," we described it as "a duality of scene." There is a slight tendentiousness here; for our characterization leans to the side of "Dublin *versus* Trieste" rather than to the side of "Dublin equals Trieste" (toward opposition rather than apposition). And when referring to the quotation from Ovid, we might rather have referred to the quoted words themselves, stressing perhaps the *original context* from which they were lifted. Thus quickly and spontaneously we smuggle inferences, or interpretations, into our report of the "factual." Yet, insofar as there is a record, there is an underlying structure of "factuality" to which we can repeatedly repair, in the hopes of hermeneutic improvement.

"Proof," then, would be of two sorts. While grounding itself in reference to the textual "facts," it must seek to make clear all elements of inference or interpretation it adds to these facts; and it must offer a rationale for its selections and interpretations. Ideally, it might even begin from different orders of "facts," and show how they led in the end to the same interpretation. We should not have much difficulty, for instance, in showing how "Dublin *versus* Trieste" could still allow for "Dublin equals Trieste," for there are respects in which Joyce's (or Stephen's!) original motives are transformed, and there are respects in which they were continued.

At the point of greatest ideal distance, an attempt to ground the analysis of literary symbolism in "terministic factuality" is to be contrasted with the analysis of symbols in terms of "analogy." If, for instance, the *word*, "tree," appears in two contexts, we would not begin by asking ourselves what rare

"symbolic" meaning a tree might have, in either religious or
psychoanalytic allegory. We would begin rather with the
literal fact that this term bridges the two contexts.

Or let us go a step further. Suppose that you *did* begin with
some pat meaning for tree, over and above its meaning as a
positive concept. (In our hypothetical case, we are assuming
that, whatever else "tree" may stand for, in these two contexts
it *at least* refers to a tree in the primary dictionary sense, as it
might not if one reference was to a "family tree.") Suppose
you were prepared to say *in advance* exactly what recondite
meaning the "image" of a tree might have, in its nature as a
"symbol" enigmatically "emblematic" of esoteric meanings.
(For instance, we could imagine a psychologist saying, "It's
not just a 'tree'; it's a father-symbol, or a mother-symbol, or in
general a parent-symbol.") Even if we granted that your
"symbolic" or "analogical" meaning for "tree" was correct, *the
fact would still remain* that the term had *one particular* set of
associates in some particular work. This is the kind of intercon-
nectedness we would watch, when studying the "facts"
of an identical *word* that recurs in changing *contexts*. Such an
investigation would be in contrast with the confining of one's
interpretation to equivalences—"analogies"—already established
even before one looks at the given text.

The "analogical" method is alluring, because by it you get
these things settled once and for all. A good literature student,
trained in the ways of indexing of "contexts" requires that each
work be studied anew, "from scratch." Night, bird, sun, blood,
tree, mountain, death? No matter, once the topic is introduced,
analogy has the answer, without ever looking further.

Part of the trouble, to be sure, comes from the fact that often
brief poems are the texts used. And the short lyric is the *most
difficult* form to explain, as its transformations are necessarily
quick, while being concealed beneath the lyric's urgent need
to establish intense unity of mood (a need so urgent that in
most lyrics the transformations are negligible, though such is
not the case with great lyrists like Keats). Long forms (epics,
dramas, novels, or poetic *sequences*) afford the most viable

material for the study of terms in changing contexts. And the principles we learn through this better documented analysis can then be applied, *mutatis mutandis,* to the study of lyric "naturalness."

Three illustrations, before proceeding:

On p. 36, in connection with the episode of Stephen's unjust punishment, we read: ". . . the swish of the sleeve of the soutane as the pandybat was lifted to strike . . ." and "the soutane sleeve swished again as the pandybat was lifted . . ." On p. 119: "Then, just as he was wishing that some unforeseen cause might prevent the director from coming, he had heard the handle of the door turning and the swish of a soutane." Here the recurrence of the swish establishes a purely "factual" bond between the two passages; and this factual bond is to be noted first as such, in its sheer terminal identity, without reference to "symbolic" or "analogical" meanings. More remotely, the "swish" might be said to *subsist* punwise in "was wishing." Hence, if this iterative verb-form were noted elsewhere in the work, one might tentatively include its context, too, as part of this grouping (made by leaps and zigzags through the narrative).

Or one may isolate this concordance: p. 73 top, citing Shelley's "Art thou pale for weariness"; p. 136, Ben Jonson's, "I was not wearier where I lay"; p. 174, in Stephen's villanelle, "Are you not weary of ardent ways?"; and on p. 175, when Stephen is watching the birds as an augury, "leaning wearily on his ashplant . . . the ashplant on which he leaned wearily . . . a sense of fear of the unknown moved in the heart of his weariness." (Ordinarily, we take it that the various grammatical forms of a word can be treated as identical. But one must always be prepared for a case where this will not be so. One could imagine a work, for instance, in which "fly" and "flight" were so used that "fly" was found to appear only in contexts meaning "soar above" or "transcend," whereas "flight" was only in contexts meaning "flee." Ordinarily, "flight" would cover both meanings, as we believe the symbol of flight does in Joyce. Or should we say that in Stephen's ecstatic vision of artistic flight the "negative" sense of *fleeing* attains rather the "positive" sense of *flying*?)

Or again: on p. 168 top, Stephen's esthetic is stated doctrinally thus: "The artist, like the god of the creation, remains within or behind or beyond or above his handiwork, invisible, refined out of existence, indifferent, paring his fingernails." Without yet asking ourselves what such paring of the nails may "symbolize," we "factually" unite this passage with ". . . . some fellows called him Lady Boyle because he was always at his nails, paring them" (p. 30 top); and (p. 32): "Mr. Gleason had round shiny cuffs and clean white wrists and fattish white hands and the nails of them were long and pointed. Perhaps he pared them too like Lady Boyle."

Such concordances are initially noted without inference or interpretation. For whereas purely terministic correlation can serve the ends of "analogical" or "symbolic" exegesis, it is far more tentative and empirical, with a constant demand for fresh inquiry. In fact, one may experimentally note many correlations of this sort without being able to fit them into an over-all scheme of interpretation.

But a grounding in the concordances of "terminal factuality" is by no means a solution to our problems.

2

If we are to begin with a "factual" index, what do we feature? Obviously, we cannot make a concordance of every book we read. And besides, even if we had a concordance before we began, we must find some principle of selection, since some terms are much more likely than others to yield good hermeneutical results. If a researcher is looking for *some particular topic*, of course, there is no problem of selection. But if the critic is attempting to characterize, in as well rounded a way as he can, the salient traits of the given work, trying to give an over-all interpretation of it as a unified symbolic act, he has a lot more to do than merely look for terminal correlations.

Almost without thinking, he will select certain *key terms.* For instance, every reader would spontaneously agree that "Stephen Dedalus" is a term to be featured. And at the very least, he would expand the name in the directions explicitly indicated by Joyce: Daedalus, Stephanoumenos, Stephaneforos.

Also, the title suggests that the critic might ask himself: "What will be the *operational* definition of 'artist' in this work?" One must be wary of titles, however. For often they were assigned or altered to meet real or imagined conditions of the market; and sometimes a work may be given a title purely for its sales value as a title, which was invented without reference to the work so entitled. In the case of the *Portrait,* of course, it would be generally agreed that the work is depicting the growth of an artist (*as so defined*) not only emotionally but in terms of a doctrine explicitly stated. For, ironically, although Stephen's doctrine denounces the "didactic" in art, it is itself as "didactic" as the Gospel; in fact it is an esthetic gospel.

But whereas the primary terms of a work operate by secondary connections, we can never be quite sure what secondary terms are likely to produce the best results. For instance, the first few lines of the book refer twice to "baby tuckoo." In a sense, this is Stephen's "real" name; for by the resources natural to narrative, an *essence* is stated in terms of *temporal* priority. Tentatively, then, we note it. And having done so, we find these possibly related entries: (p. 10 foot) "tucking the end of the nightshirt"; (p. 13) "little feet tucked up"; (p. 183) "a leather portfolio tucked under his armpit." What, then, of "Tusker Boyle" (p. 30), the unsavory fellow whom we have already mentioned in connection with the paring of his fingernails, a reference also connected with reference to the artist's "handiwork" (p. 168 top)? But the reference to hands also radiates in another direction, including both the priest's painful paddling of Stephen's hands in the pandybat episode, and the episode at the top of p. 124, where Stephen withdraws his hand from the priest as a sign that he is not to choose the religious vocation, but to become instead a "priest of the imagination." (The scene was introduced by the already cited reference to the "swish of the soutane.") This and the four references in sixteen lines to the "pain" suffered in the pandybat episode have as counterpart in the later passage an assurance that the music which had distracted him from the priest's promises dissolved his thoughts "painlessly and noiselessly."

We could radiate in many other directions. On p. 30, for instance, the reference to Tusker (or Lady) Boyle had led immediately into talk of Eileen's hands, with the memory of the time when this Protestant girl had put her hand into his pocket. Her hands "were like ivory; only soft. That was the meaning of *Tower of Ivory*," etc., whereat we can radiate to "yellow ivory" and "mottled tusks of elephants," on p. 138.

We could go on. But already we glimpse how, without our asking ourselves just what any of our bridging terms may mean "analogically" or "symbolically," a circle of terminal interrelationships is beginning to build up. And even though we might abandon some positions under pressure (as for instance the series "tuckoo-tucking-Tusker-tusks"), we find connections of similar import being established by many other routes, most of them not requiring us to do any punwise "joycing" of terms (though we might at least be justified in applying such tentatives to even early work by Joyce, in the likelihood that his later typical susceptibilities were already emerging).

But let us get back to our more immediate problem. What *should* have been indexed in the opening pages? There was a "moocow" ("symbolically" maternal?), there was a father with a "hairy face," there is a progression from "baby tuckoo" to "moocow" to "Betty Byrne" (beddy burn?!) to "lemon platt" (which puzzles us, except insofar as it may be yellow, anent which more anon). There are some *childishly* distorted jingles; and these may so set the rules of this *adult* work that we can look tentatively for such distortion *as a principle*, operating perhaps over and above the examples explicitly given in the text. (Otherwise put: if these paragraphs are *under the sign of* such punwise distortion, might we not be justified in asking whether there could also be *displaced* distortion, such as would be there if *particular* distortions were taken to stand for more than themselves, indicating that a *principle* of distortion was operating *at this point?* We bring up the possibility, to suggest *methodological* reasons why we might experimentally so pun on "Betty Byrne" as we did. We would remind our reader, however, that *we are as yet committed to nothing,* so far as this text goes. *In advance,* we make allowance for a *latitudinarian* range—as contrasted with those who, in advance, have it *all sewed up.* But we need not yet make decisions.)

Should we have noted that "His mother had a nicer smell than his father"? In any case, there are many other references to smell (pp. 10, 12, and 14, for instance); and the passage becomes doubly interesting when, in his stage of contrition (p. 116) Stephen has trouble mortifying his sense of smell: "To mortify his smell was more difficult as he found in himself no instinctive repugnance to bad odours," etc.

Where do we start? Where do we stop?

Let us admit: there must be a certain amount of waste motion here, particularly if one undertakes an index before having a fairly clear idea of a book's developments. One is threatened with a kind of methodic demoralization—for anything might pay off. Yet by an "index" we most decidedly do *not* mean such lists (by author or topic) as one finds in the back of a book. In fact, whereas an index is normally made by entries on a set of cards which are then rearranged alphabetically, we must allow our entries to remain "in the order of their appearance." For a purely alphabetical reordering makes it almost impossible to inspect a work in its *unfoldings.* And we must keep on the move, watching both for static interrelationships and for *principles of transformation* whereby a motive may progress from one combination through another to a third, etc.

Over and above whatever we may enter in our index, there will be the search for "stages." Methodologically, such a search implies a theory of "substance." That is, in contrast with those "semantic" theories which would banish from their vocabulary any term for "substance," we must believe above all in the reasonableness of "entitling." Confronting a complexity of details, we do not confine ourselves merely to the detailed tracing of interrelationships among them, or among the ones that we consider outstanding. We must also keep prodding ourselves to attempt answering this question: "Suppose you were required to find an over-all title for this entire batch of particulars. What would that be?"

The *Portrait* is in five parts, which are merely numbered. What, then, should their titles be, if they had titles? We say that such a question implies a grounding in the term, "substance," or in the furtive *function* indicated by that term, because it implies that all the disparate details included under one head are infused with a common spirit, or purpose, *i.e.*, are *consubstantial*. We may be in varying degrees right or wrong, as regards the substance that we impute to a given set of details. But they are ultimately organized with relation to one another by their joint participation in a unitary purpose, or "idea." In brief, we must keep hypothetically shifting between the particular and the general.

True: you can take it for granted that, once such a range is available, you can always attain *some* level of generalization in terms of which disparate details might be substantially related. Ideally, one seeks for terms that account for kinship not only with regard to tests of consistency; one also wants to place *sequences, developments,* showing why the parts are *in precisely that order and no other*; and if one seeks to be overthorough here, the excess should be revealed by trouble in finding cogent rationalizations.

Often, for instance, the critic may be overzealous in trying to show how a whole plot may unfold from some original situation, somewhat like an artificial Japanese flower unfolding in water. But an accurate analysis would have to show how a series of *new steps* was needed, to carry the work from its opening "germ" to its final "growth." Thus, some opening imagery might be said to contain the later plot "in germ."

(We have seen this very *Portrait* so analyzed.) But on closer analysis you will find that the opening imagery "pointed to" the ultimate destination of the plot only in the sense that, if one makes a sweep of the hand from south-southwest to north-northwest, one has thereby "implicitly" pointed due west. Critics who would analyze a book as an unfolding from an all-inclusive implication will need to use a different kind of dialectic as well. They will need to show by what successive stages a work is "narrowed down"; for its "unfolding" will be rather like a definition that begins with too broad a category, and gradually imposes strictures until the subject is "pin-pointed" (as with the game of Twenty Questions).

In the case of the *Portrait,* whatever difficulties we might have in deciding how we would specifically treat any of the details in Part I, we could "idealize" the problem in general terms thus: we note that this work leads up to the explicit propounding of an Esthetic (a doctrine, catechism, or "philosophy" of art). Then we ask how each of the parts might look, as seen from this point of view. The first part deals with rudimentary sensory perception, primary sensations of smell, touch, sight, sound, taste (basic bodily feelings that, at a later stage in the story, will be methodically "mortified"). And there is our answer. Lo! the *Esthetic* begins in simple *aisthesis.* So, in this sense, the entire first chapter could be entitled "Childhood Sensibility." It will "render" the basic requirement for the artist, as defined by the terms (and their transformations) in this particular work. It depicts the kind of personality, or temperament, required of one who would take this course that leads to the Joycean diploma (to a chair spiritually endowed by Joycean Foundations). Family relations, religion, and even politics are thus "esthetically" experienced in this opening part—experienced not as mature "ideas," or even as adolescent "passions," but as "sensations," or "images."

But whereas we would thus entitle the first section of the *Portrait,* we do not want our whole argument to depend upon this one particular choice. We are here interested mainly in the attempt to illustrate the *principle* we are discussing. We might further note that, though "Childhood Sensibility" as a title fits *developmentally* into the story as a whole, it does *not* suggest a logic of development *within* the single chapter it is intended to sum up. It merely provides a term for describing *self-consistency* among the details of the chapter. It names them solely in terms of "repetitive" form, so far as their relation to one another is concerned. And only when treating them *en bloc*, with relation to the entire five chapters, do we suggest a measure of "progressive" form here. Ideally, therefore, we should also ask ourselves into what substages (with appropriate titles) this chapter on "Childhood Sensibility" should in turn be divided. At least, when indexing, we keep thus resurveying, in quest of developments. (The thought also suggests why an index arranged alphabetically would conceal too much for our purposes.)

The very rigors of our stress upon "terminal factuality" as the ideal beginning quickly force us to become aware of this step from particulars to generalizings (a step the exact nature of which is often concealed beneath terms like "symbol" and "analogy") Hypothetically, even in a long work there might be no significant literal repeating of key terms. (We have heard tell of some ancient Chinese *tour de force* in which, though it is a work of considerable length, no single character is repeated. And one would usually be hardpressed for a wide range of literal repetitions in individual lyrics, though the quest of "factually" joined contexts usually yields good results where we have an opportunity to study a poet's terminology as maintained through several poems.) And even with the Joyce *Portrait*, which abounds in factually related contexts, we confront a notable place where we would obviously accept suicidal restrictions if we refused to take the generalizing or idealizing step from particulars to principles (or, in this case, from particular *words* to the more general *themes* or *topics* that these words signify).

We have in mind Stephen's formula for his artistic jesuitry, "silence, exile, and cunning." "Silence" yields good results, even factually. It is a word that appears at all notable moments along the road of Stephen's development up to the pronouncing

Fact, Inference and Proof

of his esthetic creed. There are a few references to cunning, the most pointed being this passage on p. 144 (all italics ours, to indicate terms we consider focal here):

> Stephen saw the *silent* soul of a jesuit look out at him from the pale loveless eyes. Like Ignatius he was lame but in his eyes burned no spark of Ignatius' enthusiasm. Even the legendary *craft* of the company, a *craft* subtler and more *secret* than its fabled books of *secret* subtle wisdom, had not fired his soul with the energy of apostleship. It seemed as if he used the shifts and lore and *cunning* of the world, as bidden to do, for the greater glory of God, without *joy* in their handling or hatred of that in them which was evil but turning them, with a firm gesture of obedience, back upon themselves; and for all this *silent service* it seemed as if he loved not at all the master and little if at all, the ends he *served*.

The references to "service" touch upon the *non serviam* theme that emerged so startlingly in the sermon. And the silence-exile-cunning formula (p. 194) had been immediately preceded by Stephen's challenge, "I will not serve," etc. We here see "cunning" and "silence" interwoven quite "factually." Also, we see the references to "craft" that could lead us into the final theme (patronymically punning) of the labyrinthine "artificer."

Yet "artificer" is not literally (thus not "factually") identical with "craft." And as for "exile": unless we missed some entries (and we may have!) the particular word does not appear elsewhere in this text. However, even assuming that we are correct, a punctiliousness bordering on "methodological suicide" would be required to keep us from including, under the *principle* of "exile," Stephen's question, "Symbol of departure or loneliness?" (p. 176), when he is considering the augury of the birds that stand for his new vocation. And once we can equate "exile" with *aloneness* (and *its* kinds of secrecy, either guilty or gestatory) we open our inquiry almost to a frenzy of entries: For "alone," in this story of a renegade Catholic boy who "forges"[2] a vocation somehow also under the aegis of a Protestant girl's hands, is as typical as any adjective in the book. Whereupon we find reasons to question

[2] (p. 199) "To forge in the smithy of my soul the uncreated conscience of my race"; (p. 131) "A hawklike man flying sunward above

whether the *apparent* disjunction (departure *or* loneliness) is really a disjunction at all. Far from their being antitheses in this work, the difference between them is hardly that between a bursting bud and a newly opened blossom.

In sum, once you go from "factual" word to a theme or topic that would include *synonyms* of this word, you are on the way to including also what we might call "operational synonyms," words which are synonyms in this particular text though they would not be so listed in a dictionary. That is, not only would a word like "stillness" be included under the same head as "silence," but you might also include here a silent *gesture* that was called "the vehicle of a vague speech," particularly as it is a scene in which we are explicitly told that he "stood silent" (pp. 76-77). Or, otherwise put: similarly, variants of "loneliness" *and* "departure" (hence even the theme of the flying bird) might be classed with "exile." And "cunning" in being extended to cover the artistic "craft," might thus expand not only into Daedalian, labyrinthine artifice, "maze," etc., but also into that doctrinal circle the center of which is the term, "imagination." We would then need some summarizing term, such as "the Joycean artist," or "the hawkman motive," to include under one head the "fact" that "silence," "exile," and "cunning" are *trinitarian* terms, which in turn are themselves linked sometimes dictionarywise (as synonyms), and sometimes "operationally" (in terms of contexts interconnected roundabout).[3]

Clearly, in the analysis of short lyrics where terms cannot be repeated in many contexts, one spontaneously looks for what

---

the sea, a prophecy of the end he had been born to serve . . . a symbol of the artist forging anew in his workshop out of the sluggish matter of the earth a new soaring impalpable imperishable being"; (p. 139) "The monkish learning, in terms of which he was trying to forge out an esthetic philosophy." (Incidentally, we would watch a word like "force," on the chance that it may turn out to be a punwise, furtive variant of "forge.")

　[3] Any connection by synonyms should always be watched for the possibility of a lurking antithesis. That is, words on their face synonymous may really *function* as antitheses in a given symbol-system. Conversely, words *apparently* "as different as day and night" may be

the old rhetoric called "amplification," some theme or topic that is restated in many ways, no single one of which could be taken as a sufficient summing up. (Here again, ideally, we might try to find working subtitles for each stanza, as a way of aggressively asking ourselves whether we can honestly say that the lyric really does get ahead, even while pausing to summarize attitudinally.)

In essentializing by entitlement, one again confronts the usual range of choices between some particular of plot or situation and some wide generalization. Specifically, for instance, we might have chosen to call the first chapter "The Pandybat," since the artist's sensitivity is built plotwise about this as its crowning incident. The second stage (marking the turn from childhood sensibility to youthful passion) is built about the logic of "The Fall," the incident in which the chapter terminates. With this title, it so happens, there is no need to decide whether we are being particular or general, or even whether we are discussing content or form. (Ideally, working titles are best when they simultaneously suggest both the gist of the story as such and the developmental stage in the purely formal sense.) We say the "logic" of the fall, as in this work the fall is a *necessary* stage in the development of the esthetic. Thus, later, p. 158, Stephen says, "The soul is born . . . first

------

but operational concealments of a *single* motive. The apparent contrast between "male" and "female," for instance, is often better analyzable as "active" and "passive" aspects of a single motive operating reflexively. And words that are synonyms on their face may be found to conceal a distinction of *attitude* that is not "natural" to a language generally. For instance, "realm" and "region" might be so distinguished that "realm" was on the "heavenly" side while "region" inclined towards the "hellish." We believe that all writers have idiosyncratic usages of this sort, their works having a greater *poetic* consistency than is *rhetorically* apparent. Indeed, we incline to suspect that all good works have "consistency to spare," so far as purely rhetorical reception is concerned, at least when one is asked about the possible rhetorical appeal of some particular internal relationship that was not noted until lengthy critical analysis had disclosed it. But only through an "excess" of such consistency (we suspect) can a work hope to have "consistency enough" for the job of wholly establishing the desired attitude in the reader.

in those moments I told you of." And we shall later try to indicate, indexwise, with what thoroughness the work interweaves its terms to this end.

Surely, the third chapter should be called "The Sermon." For that ironic masterpiece of rhetorical amplification is clearly the turning point of the chapter. To say as much, however, is to make a discovery about the form of this novel. For though the culmination of the sermon is close even to the mathematical center of the book (on p. 101 of a 199 page text we come to the "last and crowning torture of all tortures . . . the eternity of hell"), there is a very important sense in which the peripety is reserved for Chapter IV, which we might call "The New Vocation." We shall later try to show how thorough a crisis there may have been in Chapter III, in Stephen's emotions following the sermon, as revealed in the study of the Joycean esthetic. Meanwhile, we may recall that, when the choice between religion and art is finally made, it is a qualified choice, as art will be conceived in terms of theology secularized. Following Joycean theories of the emblematic image, we might also have called Chapter IV "Epiphany"; for in Stephen's vision of the bird-girl the symbol of his new vocation is made manifest. Chapter V might then be called "The New Doctrine," for we here get the catechistic equivalent of the revelation that forms the ecstatic end of Chapter IV.

When an author himself provides subtitles (and thus threatens to deprive the critic of certain delightful exercisings) at least the critic can experimentally shuttle, in looking for particular equivalents where the titles are general, and *vice versa*. But though all such essentializing by entitlement helps force us to decide what terms we should especially feature in our index, there are other procedures available.

3

First, let us consider a somewhat nondescript procedure. Some notations seem more likely than others to keep critical observation centrally directed. We list these at random:

Note all striking terms for acts, attitudes, ideas, images, relationships.

Note oppositions. In the *Portrait*, of course, we watch particularly anything bearing upon the distinction between art and religion. And as usual with such a dialectic, we watch for shifts whereby the oppositions become appositions. Stephen's secularizing of theology, for instance, could not be adequately interpreted either as a flat rejection of theological thought or as a continuation of it. Stephen has what Buck Mulligan in *Ulysses* calls "the cursed jesuit strain . . . only it's injected the wrong way." And it could be classed as another variant of the many literary tactics reflecting a shift from the religious passion to the romantic (or sexual) passion (the extremes being perhaps the varied imagery of self-crucifixion that characterizes much nineteenth-century literary Satanism).

Pay particular attention to beginnings and endings of sections or subsections. Note characteristics defining transitional moments. Note *breaks* (a point to which we shall return later, as we believe that, following the sermon, there is a notable stylistic break, a notable interruption of the continuity, even though Joyce's artistry keeps it from being felt as an outright violation of the reader's expectations already formed).

Watch names, as indicative of essence. (*Cf. numen, nomen, omen.*) In one's preparatory index, it is permissible to "joyce" them, for heuristic purposes, by even extreme punwise transformations. Not just from "dedalus" to "daedalus," for instance. But, why not even "dead louse," in view of the important part that the catching and rolling of the louse played (pp. 182-183) in Stephen's correcting of a misremembered quotation that contained the strategic word, "fall"? (The context has, besides "falls" twice in the quoted line, "falling" twice, "dying falling" once, "fall" once, and "fell" twice. But though Stephen likens himself to a louse, it is the louse that falls this time. He himself is already imbued with the spirit of Daedalian flight, whereby his fall has become transformed into a rise.)

Experimental tinkering with names does not in itself provide *proof* of anything. (So keep it a secret between us and the index). But it does suggest lines of inquiry, by bringing up new possibilities of internal relationship. On p. 167, for instance, when explaining his esthetic doctrine, Stephen says: "If a man hacking in fury at a block of wood . . . make there an image of a cow, is that cow a work of art?" Whereat we might recall not only the reference to cow with which this work began, but also the figure of the dead adolescent lover of Gabriel's wife in Joyce's story, "The Dead." Even the hint of "ivory" is found there (the step from Tusker-Lady Boyle to Tower-of-Ivory Eileen) in Gabriel's suspicion that his wife had had a clandestine meeting with Furey when ostensibly she "wanted to go to Galway with that Ivors girl." We should also recall that the story ends on a paragraph in which the word, "falling," appears no less than seven times, in the final ecstatic "epiphany" of the snow "falling softly . . . softly falling . . . falling faintly . . . faintly falling." (There was another notable reference to "falling" in this story. When Gabriel and his wife are about to enter the hotel room where he hopes to enjoy a kind of second honeymoon, the narrative states: "In the silence Gabriel could hear the falling of the molten wax into the tray," etc. The reference is to a "guttering" and "unstable" candle.) The possible fury-Furey tie-up is thus seen to have brought us by another route to the "logic of the fall" that is so important an aspect of Stephen's esthetic.[4]

[4] In an essay, "Three Definitions" (*The Kenyon Review,* Spring, 1951) we suggest the possibility that "Michael Furey" stands for a "dead" adolescent self that was an aspect of the same motives as Gabriel represented in a much later stage of development. Thus, in a sense, it would be *his own rivalry* that Gabriel was jealous of. We went on to indicate how the final imaginal merging of "living" and "dead" resolved this conflict. We also proceeded to indicate how such psycho-logistic interpretations would not be "ultimate" or "prior." And we suggested *formal* considerations whereby the story might even be considered as solving in *narrative* terms much the same problem that Kant solves philosophically in his distinction between the "conditioned" and the "unconditioned." Note, however, that just as we would break "analogy" and "symbolism" into such piecemeal problems, and would not offer "myth" as a solution here (that is, would not reduce this work

While watching for the expressions that best name a given character's number, watch also for incidental properties of one character that are present in another. Such properties in common may provide insight into the ways whereby figures on their face disparate are to be treated as different manifestations of a common motive.

Note internal forms. While noting them in their particularity, try also to conceptualize them. For instance, here's a neat job for someone who believes as much in the discipline of literary analysis as a mathematician believes in his mathematics: on pp. 182-183, conceptualize the steps from the misremembered line, "Darkness falls from the air," to the correction, "Brightness falls from the air." Of course, there are good memorizers who could reproduce the stages for you word for word. But there is a sense in which such accurate memory is itself "unprincipled," being not much more rational than a mechanical recording of the passage.

Watch for a point of *farthest internality*. We believe that in the *Portrait* this point occurs just after the sermon, most notably in the circular passage (p. 105 top) beginning, "We knew perfectly well of course," . . . and ending "We of course knew perfectly well," with its center in the expression, "endeavouring to try to induce himself to try to endeavour."

Note details of *scene* that may stand "astrologically" for motivations affecting character, or for some eventual act in which that character will complete himself. When such correspondences eventualize, they afford us sharper insight into the *steps* of a work, on its road from emergence to fulfillment. The best illustration we have for this rule is in the first chapter of Conrad's *Victory*. There has been talk of Heyst living on an island "as if he were perched on the highest peak of the Himalayas," for "an island is but the top of a mountain" (an expression which we indexed, as the author himself so pointedly

---

simply to the "myth of Daedalus" or the "Faustian myth" or even the "Christian myth"), so we do not reduce the work to purely "philosophic" terms (as though narrative were but a way of saying roundabout what philosophy can say directly).

made the "equation" for us); then the description proceeds thus:

> His nearest neighbour—I am speaking now of things showing some sort of animation—was an indolent volcano which smoked faintly all day with its head just above the northern horizon, and at night levelled at him, from among the clear stars, a dull red glow, expanding and collapsing spasmodically like the end of a gigantic cigar puffed at intermittently in the dark. Axel Heyst was also a smoker; and when he lounged out on his verandah with his cheroot, the last thing before going to bed, he made in the night the same sort of glow and of the same size as that other one so many miles away.

We could hardly fail to note so "empathic" an image, whereby an object far distant was enigmatically "equated" with a near personal property of an agent (the construct giving us a particularly ingenious kind of scene-agent ratio). And this entry later "pays off" handsomely, of course, as this same volcano breaks into agitation coincidentally with the plot's eruption into crisis. (This conformity between act and scene is not explained "rationally," as were the plot to have been shaped directly by the condition of the volcano. Rather, it serves the function of "rhetorical amplification," by restating in *scenic* terms the quality of the action that takes place with that scene as characteristic background. It is like an interpretative comment upon the action, almost a kind of "natural chorus.")

Another instance of the same sort occurs shortly after the beginning of Part II, with the description of the scene in which Heyst has his first fatal meeting with Lena:

> The Zangiacomo band was not making music; it was simply murdering silence with a vulgar, ferocious energy. One felt as if witnessing a deed of violence; and that impression was so strong that it seemed marvellous to see the people sitting so quietly on their chairs, drinking so calmly out of their glasses, and giving no signs of distress, anger or fear.

Particularly we note such a moment because it characterizes a "first," the time when Heyst and Lena first meet. And we later see that it "astrologically" foretold the quality of the action that would eventuate from this meeting. Such "foreshadowing" is standard. But when we extend the same principle for subtler inquiry, we are admonished to make a special noting of all first appearances (if only noting no more than the page number, on the possibility that a later survey of all these moments might reveal internal terministic consistencies not originally perceived).

In particular, one should note expressions marking secrecy, privacy, mystery, marvel, power, silence, guilt. Such terms are likely to point in the direction of central concerns in all cultures. Here also we might include terms for *order,* since the pyramidal nature of order brings us close to relations of "superiority" and "inferiority," with the many kinds of tension "natural" to social inequality. Such observations lead us in turn to watch for the particular devices whereby the given work "states a policy" with regard to a society's typical "problems." Here we seek hints for characterizing the work as a "strategy."

In general, we proceed by having in mind four "pyramids" or "hierarchies": (1) the pyramid of language, which allows for a Platonist climb from particulars toward "higher orders of generalization"; (2) the social pyramid, with its more or less clearly defined ladder of classes and distinctions; (3) the "natural" or "physical" pyramid (headed in such perspectives as the Darwinian genealogy); (4) the "spiritual" pyramid ("celestial" or "supernatural"). The social and linguistic pyramids are "naturally" interwoven, we take it, as language is a social product. And since the empirically linguistic is properly our center of reference when analyzing secular literary texts, we watch for ways whereby the "natural" and "supernatural" pyramids more or less clearly reflect the structure of the sociolinguistic pair.

In so doing, we do not necessarily deny that there are "natural" or "supernatural" orders, existing in their own right. We merely note that both, the one "beneath" *ideas,* the other "above" *ideas,* will necessarily be expressed in terms that reflect the *ideological* structures indigenous to the social and linguistic orders. In this sense, both "natural" and "supernatural" may be analyzable as sociolinguistic "pageantry" (by which we refer to the communicative ways, the cults of parade, exhibition, or appeal, that typify man as the typically symbolusing animal).

As all this adds up to what we might call the "hierarchal psychosis," we ask how such a psychosis might be undergoing a "cure," or "purge," within the terms of the given work, considered as a terminology. We can expect many variants of such symbolic cure; for man, as the typically symbol-using species, is naturally rich in such resources. So our thoughts about hierarchal tension lead us to watch for modes of *catharsis,* or of *transcendence,* that may offer a symbolic solution *within the given symbol-system of the particular work we are analyzing.*

We are even willing to look for ways whereby the artistic strategy that is a "solution" may serve to reestablish the very tension it is resolving. Or, if that way of stating the case seems too ironic, let us watch at least for cathartic devices whereby a rising (as seen from one angle) is a fall (as seen from another), whereby, lo! a "fall" can be a "rise." The possibility is of great importance in the case of the *Portrait,* the "factual" analysis of which *explicitly* depicts a *fall* in terms of a *soaring above.* Note, in particular, this passage (p. 125):

He would fall. He had not yet fallen but he would fall silently, in an instant. Not to fall was too hard, too hard; and he felt the silent lapse of his soul, as it would be at some instant to come, falling, falling, but not yet fallen, still unfallen, but about to fall.

Recall that this passage marks, almost "sloganistically," the step intermediate between Stephen's rejection of the religious vocation and his ecstatic vision of the bird-girl who stands imaginally for his artistic vocation.

We could here add other such rules of thumb, involving questions that require us to write over again, in this one essay, the *Motivorum* books on which we have been for some time engaged. But we finally hit upon one basic principle that might cut across all such a *gatherum omnium,* and might be argued for even if the reader did not agree with anything we have said up to this point. It is based upon an "entelechial" mode of thought. And we consider it in our next section.

4

By the "entelechial" test, we have in mind this principle: look for *moments* at which, in your opinion, the work comes to *fruition.* Imbue yourself with the terminology of these moments. And spin from them. Thus, at the very least, you would have the "epiphany" near the end of Chapter IV to guide you:

A girl stood before him in midstream; alone and still, gazing out to sea. She seemed like one whom magic had changed into the likeness of a strange and beautiful seabird. Her long slender bare legs were delicate as a crane's and pure save where an emerald trail of seaweed had fashioned itself as a sign upon the flesh. Her thighs, fuller and softhued as ivory, were bared almost to the hips where the white fringes of her drawers were like feathering of soft white down. Her slate-blue skirts were kilted boldly about her waist and dovetailed behind her. Her bosom was a bird's, soft and slight, slight and soft as the breast of some darkplumaged dove. But her long fair hair was girlish: and girlish, and touched with the wonder of mortal beauty, her face.

. . . .

—Heavenly God! cried Stephen's soul, in an outburst of profane joy.—

He turned away from her suddenly and set off across the strand. His cheeks were aflame; his body was aglow; his limbs were trembling. On and on and on he strode, far out over the sands, singing wildly to the sea, crying to greet the advent of the life that had cried to him.

Her image had passed into his soul for ever and no word had broken the holy silence of his ecstasy. Her eyes had called him and his soul had leaped at the call. To live, to err, to fall, to triumph, to recreate life out of life! A wild angel had appeared to him, the angel of mortal youth and beauty, an envoy from the fair courts of life, to throw open before him in an instant of ecstasy the gates of all the ways of error and glory. On and on and on and on!

We could continue through the next half-page that concludes the chapter. But we might better make our point by selections:

"Heard his heart in the silence . . . the tide was near the turn . . . the silence of the evening . . . closed his eyes in a languor of sleep [we forgot to list the moments of sleep and the occasions and contents of dream, among the major things to watch] . . . swooning into some new world, fantastic, dim, uncertain as under sea . . . trembling and unfolding, a breaking light, an opening flower . . . evening had fallen . . . a rim of the young moon . . . and the tide was flowing in fast to the land . . . islanding . . ."

Here, you might say, there would be many things to watch, including the word, "the," if you were argumentative enough. (And we must admit: we would not by any means say categorically that, in some structure, you could not learn more by indexing the "the's" than by any other term.)

Basically, though, you have seen the bird-girl, who is to stand for motives far beyond her nature as sheer image. So, *at the very least*, with this obvious fulfillment to guide you, you would put in your index the first implicit announcements of the bird theme, on p 2: "the eagles will come and pull out his eyes"; "the greasy leather orb flew like a heavy bird through the grey light." You do not know just how you will use these entries. You are not even sure that you will use them at all. But you note them. You would note them because of the fact that they are classed among things to do with birdness, a category experimentally broad enough to include Stephen's roommate Heron, the final reference to "old father, old artificer," the vision of the "hawklike man," and (pp. 175-176) the augury of the birds circling "from left to right," their emblematic nature defined by questionable disjunction as "symbol of departure or of loneliness." Also, as we are trying ever to see *beyond* the symbolizings in the given work even while trying to see as far as we can *into* that work's purely internal consistency, we *especially* note all *eye* terms with regard to Joyce, even beyond the eye-I pun natural to the accidents of English. And having in mind the step from "dying fallings of sweet airs" to "sucking mouths" on p. 182, we dare think also of the "blind mouths" in Milton's "Lycidas," while the reference to "scum" here throws us back to Stephen's childhood baptism in rat-infested scum (p. 7), and other incidences of this term (pp. 49, 52, 85). One should remember, for later use, that on p. 49 this scum is called "yellow": yellow turns out to be a particularly notable color, because of its specific relation to Stephen's esthetic, as we shall explain later.

If (in this same passage of "epiphany") you have noted "soft," which appears six times in six lines (p. 132 foot–p. 133 top), surely a sufficient incidence to make it experimentally notable, then you would certainly note (p. 106) the "soft language" twice so called, and equated with "stale shite" and the horrors that were "circling closer and closer to enclose." Or you would note the words linking "sin" and softness that terminate Chapter II, the chapter we have entitled "The Fall."[5]

[5] The partially involuntary fall through sexual passion at the end of Chapter II might be distinguished from the deliberate fall of Chapter IV (the choice of a new vocation) somewhat as "passive" is distinguished from "active." It is the latter that Stephen equates with Luciferian pride, epitomized in his many variants of the formula, "I will not serve." All told, the accountancy is somewhat like this: The earlier passionate fall prepared for the later vocational choice; the two were thus related as different species of a common genus (a genus also marked by such "operational synonyms" as "soft," "circling," "yellow," and "scum"). By the time the book is finished, the theme of falling has become translated into the theme of ecstatic elevation, even while retaining signs of its beginnings.

We might also note how music figures in this psychic bookkeeping. Music stands for the new motive. When turning from the Bible as doctrine, Stephen still loved it as music (p. 79). When the jesuit was proposing that he become a priest, the sound of distant music snapped the continuity (p. 124). The themes of rising and falling are interwoven with the music theme and the bird theme as the music theme itself has this design: "It seemed to him that he heard notes of fitful music leaping upwards a tone and downwards a diminishing

If you asked what the young moon meant, and took notes to find out, you would get the answer doubly, though ambiguously, on p. 176 top: "Thoth, the god of writers . . . bearing on his narrow ibis head the cusped moon. . . . He would not have remembered the god's name but that it was like an Irish oath." The reference to "profane joy" might admonish us to note the "tears of joy" and the "tremor of fear and joy" in the brothel scene (pp. 66-76). "Silence" we have already discussed. Meanwhile, beyond the sheer pattern of the turning tide (transitional scene for transitional act) we would note the further pattern in the fact that, upon seeing the girl who is henceforth to stand for his vocation, Stephen exaltedly turns *from her,* going "on and on and on."

Since the bird-girl is a "wild angel," whose presence sanctions his resolve "to live, to err, to fall" (p. 133), and since the word, "wild," appears several times in this passage of "fulfillment" which we have been experimentally examining for cues as to the terms that we might favor in our index, we watch "wild." It occurs in many notable contexts, including (p. 106) the passage where, in his terror, Stephen undergoes a purgation in the most literal, physical sense: "clasping his cold forehead wildly, he vomited profusely in agony."

But with that reference to Stephen's physical purgation, following the sermon and his almost cataleptic response to it (pp. 104-105) as he pauses in terror outside the door of his room, our inquiry could well take another turn. For immediately after the physical cleansing, a new life begins. We read that "the city was spinning about herself a soft cocoon of yellowish haze" (p. 106 foot). Yet on both pp. 76 and 77, the

---

fourth, upwards a tone and downwards a major third" (p. 127); "But the notes were long and shrill and whirring, unlike the cry of vermin, falling a third or a fourth and trilled as the flying beaks clove the air. Their cry was shrill and clear and fine and falling like threads of silken light unwound from whirring spools" (p. 175). (And, of course, when considering this purely grammatical disjunction between vermin and the new vocation, we would note rather how, so far as sheer imagery is concerned, the two themes are *brought together,* being as it were "said in the same breath.")

flames of the brothels were called "yellow." Later, when the
esthetic doctrine is being spelled out, one of Stephen's companions who participates in the definition of the doctrine is
Lynch, with his "excrementitious intellect" and his resolve
"to swear in yellow" (pp. 159, 165, etc.) Yellow is the first
color we encounter (line two) in *Ulysses*. The passage somewhat sacrilegiously equates shaving with the ministry of the
Mass. In the *Portrait*, we note how we again circle back to the
theme of Lady Boyle, since Stephen at one point (as we already noted) ponders on "yellow ivory" and the "mottled
tusks of elephants" (p. 138). Nor should we forget that the
bird-girl (p. 132 foot) had thighs "softhued as ivory." And we
can now discern how the *principle* of yellow, though not the
literal term, is lurking (p. 30) in the turn from Lady Boyle
paring his nails to the memory of Eileen, whose hands were
"like ivory; only soft."

Admittedly, our work has hardly more than begun, so far
as the study of this particular text is concerned. In particular,
for instance, we would like to have talked at some length
about the passage which we take to be the moment of farthest
internality, the "circular" paragraph at the top of p. 105. We
have tried elsewhere to show that this "break" in the structure
of the work (the sudden brief irruption of Joyce's later manner
into a narrative style otherwise traditionally realistic) can be
related to the principle of "arrest" that characterizes Stephen's
esthetic, as proclaimed in Part V. For it is precisely here that
Stephen, terrified by the sermon, pauses, unable to cross a
threshold: precisely at this moment of arrest, there leaps forth
the passage cryptically prophetic of the later manner:

—We knew perfectly well of course that although it was bound
to come to the light he would find considerable difficulty in endeavouring to try to induce himself to try to endeavour to ascertain
the spiritual plenipotentiary and so we knew of course perfectly
well—

We believe that much can be done with this "break," even
beyond the confines of the one book. But in any case, for the
time being we can note that it is another of those places where

the book comes to a kind of *ad interim* fulfillment; hence it would be another place from which our search could radiate. On the next page, for instance, it leads "factually" into talk of "circling." Stephen's doctrine itself, of course, would be another "entelechial moment" to work from, particularly if one remembered that Stephen's interlocutors in the discussion are to be taken as part of the definition. We could add a few other spots (for instance, the formula, "Silence, exile, and cunning," is a splendid fulfillment, or culminating moment). There are eight or nine such in all.

Similarly, there are places where some one word flares up like a *nova*, as we saw with regard to the word, "fall." These, too, would be watched as "fulfillments."

All told, one proceeds from such places, where the work comes to a temporary head. One radiates in search of labyrinthine internal consistency, while at the same time watching for progressions. One tries to be aware of one's shifts between "factuality" and "thematic" generalizing. One watches for over-all social tensions, and for the varying tactics of "purification" with regard to them. And one is thereby talking about "symbolism," willy-nilly.[6]

[6] We have omitted mention of one area that we tentatively call "channels of affinity." They would be to the study of Poetics what "topics" are to the study of rhetoric. But whereas the traditional "topics" were static ("places"), channels of affinity would be developmental. It is our notion that certain progressions are more "natural" than others. Thus with the progression "from Venus to Mars" or *vice versa*. Or the progression from awe to liquid light. Or from sex to food (as two basic orders of appetition). Such "naturalness" may be primarily due to the nature of the body. But it can also be a part of "second nature." For instance, one finds in our society many progressions from thought of woman to thought of the hunt, but such a double-meaning for venery is socially conditioned. We have been taking notes of this sort on a purely empirical basis. And we are still quite uncertain as to how they should be classified. Certain ones, however, recur so often, with effective results (in both serious and comic works), we do think there is something real to work on here, despite the shiftiness of the material.

From *Symbols and Values: An Initial Study* (Thirteenth Symposium of the Conference on Science, Philosophy and Religion. New York: Harper & Brothers, 1954), pp. 283-306.

Three Oratorical Poems
(1955)

For a Modernist Sermon

You'll have an eight-cylinder car in heaven—
Air conditioning—
Indirect lighting—
a tile bathroom and a white porcelain kitchen.

Despite the phenomenal growth of population,
there'll be no traffic problem,
if you would drive out
to the Garden of Eden
for a week-end.

O the celestial sundaes—
all flavors made with the purest chemicals.

No strike—no speed-up—no lay-off—
everybody a coupon-clipper in heaven,
living in peace, on the eternal drudgery
of the damned.

All will be fragrant and quiet in heaven,
like the best real estate in Westchester.
All noise and stench segregated
to the under side of the railroad.

In heaven,
When you want something,
you just fill out an order
and your want is met like magic,
from the Power-plants
   Assembly rooms
     Factories
       Presses

Forges
Mines
Mills
Smelteries
and Blast-Furnaces

of hell.

Creation Myth

In the beginning, there was universal Nothing.
Then Nothing said No to itself and thereby begat
Something,
Which called itself Yes.

Then No and Yes, cohabiting, begat Maybe.
Next all three, in a ménage à trois, begat Guilt.

And Guilt was of many names:
Mine, Thine, Yours, Ours, His, Hers, Its, Theirs—
and Order.

In time things so came to pass
That two of its names, Guilt and Order,
Honoring their great progenitors, Yes, No, and Maybe,
Begat History.

Finally, History fell a-dreaming
And dreamed about Language—

(And that brings us to critics-who-write-critiques of-
critical-criticism.)

Mercy Killing

Faithfully
We had covered the nasturtiums
Keeping them beyond
Their season

Until, farewell-minded,
Thinking of age and ailments,
And noting their lack of lustre,
I said:

"They want to die;
We should let the flowers die."

That night
With a biting clear full moon
They lay exposed.

In the morning,
Still shaded
While the sun's line
Crawled towards them from the northwest,
Under a skin of ice
They were at peace.

From *Book of Moments: Poems, 1915-1954* (Los Altos, Calif.: Hermes Publications, 1955), pp. 56-57, 5, 26.

Tautological Cycle of Terms for "Order"
(1958)

When reading this essay, and later references to the same subject, the reader might find it helpful to consult the accompanying chart—Cycle of Terms Implicit in the Idea of "Order"—outlining the "Terministic Conditions for 'Original Sin' and 'Redemption' (intrinsic to the Idea of 'Order')."

First, consider the strategic ambiguity whereby the term "Order" may apply both to the realm of nature in general and to the special realm of human sociopolitical organizations (an ambiguity whereby, so far as sheerly empirical things are concerned, a natural order could be thought to go on existing even if all human beings, with their various sociopolitical orders, were obliterated). This is a kind of logical pun whereby our ideas of the natural order can become secretly infused by our ideas of the sociopolitical order.

One might ask: Is not the opposite possibility just as likely? Might not the terms for the sociopolitical order become infused by the genius of the terms for the natural order? They do, every time we metaphorically extend the literal meaning of a natural image to the realm of the sociopolitical. It is the point that Bentham made much of, in his Theory of Fictions, his systematic procedure ("archetypation") for locating the natural images that may lurk undetected in our ideas, and so may mislead us into attempting to deal too strictly in terms of the irrelevant image. For instance, if Churchillian rhetoric gets us to thinking of international relations in such terms as "iron curtains" and "power vacuums," then we must guard lest we respond to the terms too literally—otherwise we shall not conceive of the political situation accurately enough. The nations of the Near East are no "vacuum." Theologians have made similar observations about the use of natural images to express the idea of godhead.

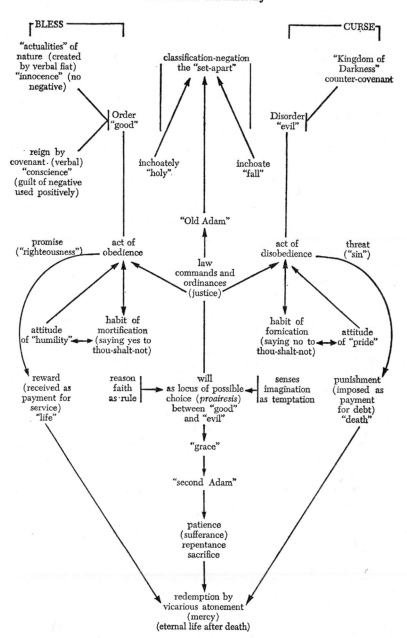

Cycle of Terms Implicit in the Idea of "Order"

God as Author and Authority

BLESS

"actualities" of
nature (created
by verbal fiat)
"innocence" (no
negative)

Order
"good"

reign by
covenant (verbal)
"conscience"
(guilt of negative
used positively)

classification-negation
the "set-apart"

CURSE

"Kingdom of
Darkness"
counter-covenant

Disorder
"evil"

inchoately
"holy"

inchoate
"fall"

"Old Adam"

promise
("righteousness")

act of
obedience

threat
("sin")

act of
disobedience

law
commands and
ordinances
(justice)

attitude
of "humility"

habit of
mortification
(saying yes to
thou-shalt-not)

habit of
fornication
(saying no to
thou-shalt-not)

attitude
of "pride"

reward
(received as
payment for
service)
"life"

reason
faith
as rule

will
as locus of possible
choice (proairesis)
between "good"
and "evil"

senses
imagination
as temptation

punishment
(imposed as
payment
for debt)
"death"

"grace"

"second Adam"

patience
(sufferance)
repentance
sacrifice

redemption by
vicarious atonement
(mercy)
(eternal life after death)

But it is much more important, for our present purposes, to spot the movement in the other direction. We need to stress how a vision of the natural order can become infused with the genius of the verbal and sociopolitical orders.

Thus, from the purely logological point of view, we note how, inasmuch as the account of the Creation in Genesis involves on each "day" a kind of enactment done through the medium of God's "Word," the sheerly "natural" order contains a verbal element or principle that from the purely empirical point of view could belong only in the sociopolitical order. Empirically, the natural order of astrophysical motion depends upon no verbal principle for its existence. But theologically it does depend upon a verbal principle. And even though one might say that God's creative fiats and his words to Adam and Eve are to be conceived as but *analogous* to ordinary human verbal communication, our point remains the same. For from the empirical point of view, there would not even be an *analogy* between natural origins and responses to the power of words. The world of natural, nonverbal motions must be empirically the kind of world that could continue with its motions even if it contained no species, such as man, capable of verbal action; and it must be described without any reference to a Creation by verbal fiat, whether or not there had been such.

By a Dramatistic ambiguity, standard usage bridges this distinction between the realms of verbal action and nonverbal motion when it speaks of sheerly natural objects or processes as "actualities." Here even in a purely secular usage we can discern a trace of the theological view that sees nature as the sign of God's action—and thus by another route we see the theological way of merging the principle of the natural order with the principles of verbal contract or covenant intrinsic to legal enactment in the sociopolitical order.

But to proceed with the "tautologies":

If, by "Order," we have in mind the idea of a command, then obviously the corresponding word for the proper response would be "Obey." Or there would be the alternative, "Disobey." Thus we have the proportion: Order is to Disorder as Obedience is to Disobedience. However, there is a logological sense in which the things of nature could be called "innocent." They cannot disobey commands, since they cannot understand commands. They do not have a "sense of right and wrong," or more generically, a "sense of yes and no." They simply do as they do—and that's that. Such would be the *non posse peccare* of natural things, or even of humans insofar as their "natural" state was not bound by moralistic negatives. All was permissive in Eden but the eating of the one forbidden fruit, the single negative that set the conditions for the Fall (since, St. Paul pointed out, only the law can make sin, as Bentham was later to point out that only the law can make crime). The Biblical myth pictures natural things as coming into being through the agency of God's Word; but they can merely do as they were designed to do, whereas with God's permission though not without his resentment, the seed of Adam can do even what it has been explicitly told not to do. The word-using animal not only understands a thou-shalt-not; it can carry the principle of the negative a step further, and answer the thou-shalt-not with a disobedient No. Logologically, the distinction between natural innocence and fallen man hinges about this problem of language and the negative. Eliminate language from nature, and there can be no moral disobedience. In this sense, moral disobedience is "doctrinal." Like faith, it is grounded in language.

"Things" can but *move* or *be moved*. "Persons" by definition can "act." In being endowed with words (symbols) by which they can frame responses to questions and commands, by the same token they have "responsibility."

Looking into the *act* of Disobedience, we come upon the need for some such term as "Pride," to name the corresponding *attitude* that precedes the act. And some such term as "Humility" names the idea of the attitude that leads into the act of Obedience.

But implicit in the distinction between Obedience and Disobedience there is the idea of some dividing line, some "watershed" that is itself midway between the two slopes. Often a word used for naming this ambiguous moment is "Will," or more fully, "Free Will," which is thought of as a faculty that makes possible the choice between the yea-saying of Humble Obedience or the nay-saying of Prideful Disobedience (the choice between *serviam* and *non serviam*).

Ontologically, and theologically, we say that this locus of freedom makes possible the kind of personal choice we have in mind when we speak of "Action." But note that, logologically, the statement should be made the other way round. That is, whereas ontologically or theologically we say that by being endowed with free will man is able to act morally, the corresponding logological statement would be: Implicit in the idea of an act is the idea of free will. (Another version of the formula would be: Implicit in the idea of an act is the idea of freedom.)

The ontological and theological statements may or may not be true. The logological statement would be "true logologically" even if it were not true ontologically. That is, even if we hypothetically suppose, with strict behaviorists and the like, that there is no such thing as "free will," that all "action" is reducible to terms of mechanical "motion," it would still remain true that implicit in the idea of action there is the idea of freedom. If one cannot make a choice, one is not acting, one is but being moved, like a billiard ball tapped with a cue and behaving mechanically in conformity with the resistances it encounters. But even if men are doing nothing more than that, the *word* "act" *implies* that they are doing more—and we are now concerned solely with the implications of terms.

As regards the Dramatistic tautology in general, an act is done by an agent in a scene. But such an act is usually preceded by a corresponding attitude, or "incipient act" (as when an act of friendliness follows a friendly attitude on the part of the agent). The scene is motivational locus of the act insofar as the act represents a scene-act ratio (as, for instance, when an "emergency situation" is said to justify an "emergency measure"). But as the act derives from an attitude of the agent, the agent-act ratio can be narrowed to an attitude-act ratio, as when a friendly agent does a friendly act. The term "Will" is apparently designed to assign a "place" to the choice between different possibilities of attitude-act development. Here a verb is thought of as a noun; the idea of "the will" as willing is conceived after the analogy of rain raining, though we do not speak of fear as fearing. But the idea of such a locus for "the Will" brings up a further problem: What in turn influences "the Will"?

On the Disorder side, this role is assigned to the Imagination, insofar as the imagination's close connection with sensory images is thought both to make it highly responsive to the sensory appetites and to make sensory appetites more enticing. In brief, the combination of Imagination and the Senses, by affecting the Will from the side of Disorder, is said to predispose towards Temptation, *except* insofar as Imagination in turn is corrected from the side of Order by the controls of Reason and Faith (which can also be thought of as having a controlling effect upon each other). Another refinement here is the notion that, once Imagination is on the side of Reason, it can contribute to Order, rather than to Disorder, by making reasonable things seem sensible, and thus inducing the Wills of persons weak in Reason to nonetheless freely choose, as it were reasonably, and thus to act on the side of Order, eschewing Temptation.

The idea of Reason, in such a system, is obviously permeated with ideas of Dominion, owing to its identification with ideas of control and as indicated in the formula, "the Rule of Reason." So it brings us clearly back to the principle of sovereignty underlying the general idea of Order by Covenant. The relation between Reason and Faith becomes ambiguous because of the possible shift between the natural order and the sociopolitical order as grounds of Reason. For if the sociopolitical Order is conceived in "ultimate" terms (as it is in the idea of a Covenant derived from God), then Faith must be a kind of control higher than Reason, insofar as Reason is identified with "Natural Law" and with purely worldly rules of governance. (Incidentally, we might note the strongly verbal element in both, as indicated by the close relation between Rational and Logical and by St. Paul's statement that the doctrines of the Faith are learned "by hearing." However, there is said to be a further stage of supernatural awareness, called by St. Anselm *contemplatio* and by Spinoza *scientia intuitiva,* which would by definition transcend the verbal.)

There is also an act-agent ratio, as with the Aristotelian notion of *hexis, habitus,* the notion that a person may develop a virtuous Disposition by the practices of virtue or a vicious Disposition by repeated indulgence in vice. And this brings us to the subtlest term of all, as regards the set of major Dramatistic terms clustering about the idea of Order; namely, Mortification.

Of all theology-tinged terms that need logological reclamation and refurbishment, this is perhaps the most crucial. Here the motives of sacrifice and dominion come to a head in everyday living. The possibility is that most ailments now said to be of "psychogenic" origin are but secularized variants of what might be called "mortification in spite of itself." That is, if we are right in assuming that governance makes "naturally" for victimage, either of others (homicidally) or of ourselves (suicidally), then we may expect to encounter many situations in which a man, by attitudes of self-repression, often causes or aggravates his own bodily and mental ills.

The derived meaning (humiliation, vexation, chagrin) would figure here. But mainly we have in mind the Grand Meaning, "subjection of the passions and appetites, by penance, abstinence, or painful severities inflicted on the body," mortification as a kind of governance, an extreme form of "self-control," the deliberate, disciplinary "slaying" of any motive that, for "doctrinal" reasons, one thinks of as unruly. In an emphatic way, mortification is the exercising of oneself in "virtue"; it is a systematic way of saying no to Disorder, or obediently saying yes to Order. Its opposite is license, *luxuria*, "fornication," saying yes to Disorder, no to Order.

The principle of Mortification is particularly crucial to conditions of empire, which act simultaneously to awaken all sorts of odd and exacting appetites, while at the same time imposing equally odd and exacting obstacles to their fulfillment. For "mortification" does not occur when one is merely "frustrated" by some external interference. It must come from within. The mortified must, with one aspect of himself, be saying no to another aspect of himself—hence the urgent incentive to be "purified" by "projecting" his conflict upon a scapegoat, by "passing the buck," by seeking a sacrificial vessel upon which he can vent, as from without, a turmoil that is actually within. "Psychogenic illness" would occur in cases in which one was scrupulous enough to deny himself such easy outgoing relief and, instead, in all sorts of roundabout ways, scrupulously circles back upon himself, unintentionally making his own constitution the victim of his hierarchally goaded entanglements. At least, that's the idea.

To complete the pattern: On the side of Order, where the natural actualities created by verbal fiat are completed in sovereignty and subjection by Covenant, with Obedience goes promise of reward (as payment for service), while on the other side goes Disobedience, with threat of punishment as enforced payment for disservice.

Then comes the Grand Rounding Out, where the principle of reward as payment (from the Order side) merges with the principle of punishment as payment (from the Disorder side), to promise of redemption by vicarious atonement. Sovereignty and subjection (the two poles of governance) are brought together in the same figure (Christ as King and Christ as Servant, respectively)—and the contradiction between these principles is logically resolved by a narrative device, the notion of two advents whereby Christ could appear once as servant and the second time as king. Here is the idea of a "perfect" victim to cancel (or "cover") what was in effect the "perfect" sin (its technical perfection residing in the fact that it was the first transgression of the first man against the first and foremost authority).

However, the symmetry of the design does not resolve the problem of the "watershed moment," the puzzle of the relation between "determinism" and "free will." The search for a cause is itself the search for a scapegoat, as Adam blames Eve, Eve blames the serpent, the serpent could have blamed Lucifer, and Lucifer could have blamed the temptations implicit in the idea of Order (the inchoate "fall" that, as we saw in the quotation from Coleridge, is intrinsic to the "creation of the non-absolute"). Adam himself has a hint of the Luciferian rejoinder when he says to the Lord God that he received the fruit from "the woman whom thou gavest to be with me." Also, from the purely imagistic point of view, there is a sense in which the Lord God has caused Adam to be tempted by an aspect of himself, in accordance with the original obstetrical paradox whereby woman was born of man.

Here would be a purely "grammatical" way of stating the case: If order, implying the possibility of disorder, implies a possible *act* of disobedience, then there must be an agent so endowed, or so minded, that such an act is possible to him—and the *motives* for such an act must eventually somehow be referred to the *scene* out of which he arose, and which thus somehow contains the principles that in their way make a "bad" act possible.

Arrived at this point, we might shift the problem of the "watershed moment" to another plane, by recalling that the same conditions of divisiveness also make for the inchoately "holy," inasmuch as the Hebrew word for "holy," *qodesh*, means literally the "separate," the "set apart," as does the word *qadesh*, which means "Sodomite." This verbal tangle has often been commented on, and it applies also to the New Testament word *hagios*, which means both "holy" and "accursed," like its Latin counterpart, *sacer*. Here, we might say, is a purely terministic equivalent of the problem of choice, or motivational slope. The question of de-terminism narrows down to a kind of term that within itself contains two slopes (two different judgments or "crises").

As regards the matter of terms, we could move into the area of personality proper by equating human personality with the ability to use symbol-systems (centering in the feeling for the negative, since "reason," in its role as the "sense of right and wrong," is but a special case of the "sense of yes and no"). Thus, more broadly, we could say that the conception of the creative verbal fiat in Genesis is essentially the *personal principle*. But insofar as personal character is defined by choice (cf. Aristotle on *proairesis, Poetics,* VI, 24), the question then becomes one of deciding how far back the grounds of choice must be traced (atop the primary logological fact that the *perfection* of choice comes to a head in the formal distinction between Yes and No). Insofar as Genesis would depict us as arising from a scene that is the act of a super-person, and insofar as redemption is thought to be got by voluntary enlistment on the side of Order, conceived sacrificially, the ultimate formula becomes that of Jeremiah 31:18: "Turn thou me, and I shall be turned" (*converte me, et convertar*). Here the indeterminate watershed of "free" choice is reducible to a question of this sort: Though all men are given enough "grace" to be saved, how can anyone be saved but by being given enough grace to be sure of using it? Yet how could he have as much saving grace as that, without in effect being *compelled* to be saved (in which case he would not, in the last analysis, have "free will")?

Fortunately, it is not our duty, as logologers, to attempt solving this ultimate theological riddle, entangled in ideas of providence, predestination, and the possibilities of an elect, chosen from among the depraved, all of whom deserve eternal damnation, but some of whom are saved by God in his mysterious mercy, and may attest to their future glory by becoming a kind of materially prosperous elite here and now (or at least by being able to answer without question).

Fortunately, as logologers, we need but consider the ways in which such ideas are interwoven with the conditions of dominion, as they prevail among human symbol-using animals. As seen in this light, the thought of all such issues leads us to revision of our initial dialectical pattern. That is, the Order-Disorder pair is not enough. And what we need now is another kind of antithesis, setting Order against Counter-Order.

Methodologically, we might say that we have now come upon the penalties resulting from our earlier decision to approach this problem in terms of "Order" rather than in terms of "Covenant." For the idea of a "Counter-Covenant" would have been somewhat different from the idea of such a mere disintegration as is usually suggested by the term "Disorder."

In sum, there is a notable qualitative difference between the idea of a mere "fall" from a position in which one still believes, but to which one is at times unequal, and the idea of a deliberate turn to an alternative allegiance. It would be a difference between being "weak in virtue" and being "strong in sin."

But perhaps we should try to sum up the line of reasoning we have been pursuing in these last paragraphs. We have been considering the problem of a possible ultimate ground for "Temptation." Logologically, "Temptation" is but a tautological aspect of the idea of "Order." It is grounded in the idea of a verbal command, which by its very nature contains possibilities of both obedience and disobedience. We do not "command" the nonverbalizing things of nature. To the best of our ability, we simply set up conditions which we think likely to bring about the kind of situation we desire. We reserve our commands (or requests!) for language-using entities that can, to varying degrees, resist. And the command is backed, explicitly or implicitly, by promises or threats.

However: ontologically, or theologically, such a purely "tautological" point of view would not be enough. And we confront such problems as St. Augustine was concerned with in his battles with the Manichaeans. We may, like the Manichaeans, conceive of an ultimate Tempter, existing in his own right and with powers rivaling those of God. Or we may derive everything from a God who is by definition merciful, and good, the author of a wholly good Creation, yet who not only lets man sin, but permits the existence and incessant schemings of a supernatural tempter endowed with diabolical ingenuity and persuasiveness. Hence arises the "problem of evil" (as with Augustine's urgent question, "*Unde malum?*"). We have considered in the previous talk how Augustine proposed to solve the problem theologically by his notion of evil as a "deficient cause," a kind of "eclipse."

But logologically, the question takes on a different form. Logologically, moral "evil" is a species of *negative*, a purely linguistic (or "rational") principle. And insofar as natural calamities are viewed in terms of moral retribution, we should say that the positive events of nature are being seen through the eyes of moral negativity (another instance of ways whereby the genius of the verbal and sociopolitical orders can come to permeate our ideas of the natural order). All told, "evil" is implicit in the idea of "Order" because "Order" is a polar, or dialectical term, implying an idea of "Disorder."

But there can be two kinds of "Disorder": (1) a tendency towards failure to obey completely always; (2) disobedience due to an out-and-out enrollment in the ranks of a rival force. We might call this a distinction between mere Disorder and deliberate allegiance to a Counter-Order. (There is an analogous situation in contemporary politics, since a person's disagreements with those in authority may be interpreted either as temperamental deviation from the prevailing orthodoxy or as sinister, secret adherence to an organized enemy alien power.)

Theologically, perhaps the analogous distinction would be between the kind of "Temptation" that is intrinsic to the possibility of choice and the kind that attains its ideal perfection in the notion of a Faustian pact with the Devil—the difference between ordinary "backsliding" and "heresy" or "black magic." In Joyce's Portrait, it would correspond to the distinction between Stephen's sexual fall despite himself in the second section, and his deliberate choice of a "proud" esthetic calling, as "priest of the imagination," in section four. Problems of "predestination" lie in the offing, inasmuch as different people are differently tempted or differently enlightened, and such differences are not of their own choosing but arise in connection with the accidents of each man's unique, particular destiny. (In the *Confessions,* for instance, we see St. Augustine interpreting as God's will many decisions which he had made for quite different personal reasons. And no man could sell his soul to the Devil, if God—who was necessarily present at the signing of the contract—but chose that moment to flood the victim's imagination with the full realization of his danger.)

From *The Rhetoric of Religion: Studies in Logology* (Boston: Beacon Press; copyright © 1961 by Kenneth Burke), pp. 183-196.

The Principle of Composition
(1961)

For our point of departure here, let's use Poe's essay, *The Philosophy of Composition,* where he gives his suspect account of the way in which he wrote *The Raven.* According to Poe (and few if any readers have seemed inclined to believe him) no point in the composition of the poem "is referable to accident or intuition." And his essay was designed to demonstrate "that the work proceeded, step by step, to its completion with the precision and rigid consequence of a mathematical problem."

I. A. Richards has referred to Poe's explanation as "an ostentatious parade of allegedly perfect adjustment of selected means to fully foreseen ends." (Cf. "Poetic Process and Literary Analysis," in *Style and Language,* edited by Thomas A. Sebeok.) Further: "Poe, so eager—in Harry Levin's phase—'to convince the world of his self-mastery,' spares no pains to make this clear." And he concludes: "However 'The Raven' may in fact have been written, we know that most poems are not composed so; the author's manuscripts, where first drafts are available, at least show us that."

It's not unlikely that Poe could at least have come closer to the logically deductive procedures he retails than would ordinarily be the case. After all, he was the author of works like *The Gold-Bug.* And there's no reason to deny that such "stories of ratiocination" do require a kind of planning not unlike the series of logical deductions by which, according to Poe, he decided upon the length of the poem, its subject matter, its contrasts, its tone, its refrain, etc., etc. When planning stories of this sort, "It is only with the *dénouement* constantly in view that we can give a plot its indispensable air of consequence, or causation, by making the incidents, and especially the tone at all points, tend to the development of the intention." Author and reader here reverse things. Beginning with the solution, the author figures out the kind of situation that would require such a solution. But the reader proceeds in the other direction, by beginning with the problem and gradually progressing towards the solution. So a kind of "deductive" planning is involved in such stories, at least. And Poe himself (in a letter referring to both "the bird" and "the bug" in the same breath) spontaneously indicates that *The Raven* and *The Gold-Bug* were for him classifiable in the same bin.

There are many kinds of story, and many kinds of poem, which might conceivably be written from hand to mouth, from pillar to post, the writer himself not sure exactly where he is going until he gets there. But it's almost inconceivable that a story of ratiocination like *The Gold-Bug* could be written thus. Here the art is like that of a Houdini. Houdini didn't let the public set the conditions from which he should escape. Rather, having hit upon the device that would permit him to escape, he next figured out the exact conditions of confinement which would make such a means of escape possible. In brief, from his idea of the *dénouement* he deduced his ideas of the prior complications.

However, my concern with a possible similarity of motives between the poem of the bird and the story of the bug does not require me to believe Poe's account of how he wrote the poem. As regards our present speculations, it doesn't matter whether Poe was telling the literal truth or a barefaced lie. In fact, to get the point I am after, let's assume that Poe's account was a fabrication from the whole cloth—and that it was done either by way of showmanship or (as Harry Levin's effective belowthebeltism seems to suggest) to supply a formal, public denial of the author's notorious personal weaknesses. For the present, we'll pass up the personal motives that may have figured in the rationalizing of his project when, having decided that the ideal topic of his poem must somehow combine death and beauty, he brought forth his crucial formula: "The death, then, of beautiful woman is, unquestionably, the most poetical topic in the world." Whatever may be our speculations on this point with regard to Poe's poetically necrophile tendencies (as though he were proved to have been an undertaker who lost his license for morbid reasons) the question need not detain us here. Our question is: What could be said in favor of Poe's procedure in his essay on *The Raven*, even if (to make our case as clear as possible) we flatly assume that his account of how he wrote the poem is completely false?

First, let's dispose of the most likely alternative: the "historical," "biographical," or temporally "genetic" account of a work's development. Here would be the hit-and-run, catch-as-catch-can record of the poem in its various stages of planning and revision. The primary evidence for such a study of poetic composition is usually taken to be various drafts of the given work, arranged as far as possible in the order of their production. Often the inspection of such material does give us new insight into the author both as a personality and as a craftsman. However, we must remember that: Even if we had a record of every such single step involved in the actual writing of a poem, of the exact order in which revisions were made, of the author's dreams and personal quandaries during the writing, of his borrowings from other authors or from situations in life itself (unrelated incidents that happen to occur at the time when the work was being produced and that the author found ways of transforming for the particular purposes of his poem)—even if we had a mountain of such data, we should have but a fraction of the information needed to chart fully the work's genesis. For obviously, if a poem is worth the trouble of a second look, the germ of its beginnings had been planted long before the stage of actual writing. In this sense, the poet began "planning" his poem (consciously or unconsciously) many years before he got around to the writing of it. An inspection of successive drafts, notebooks, the author's literary habits in general, etc., helps—but in the last analysis the poem's universe of discourse dissolves into the mystery of the universe itself.

However, though studies of this sort can't possibly go deep enough, they do provide us with a high-class kind of gossip that is often worth the effort. My point is not that such pursuits should be neglected, but simply that they do not replace the "principle" involved in Poe's essay. And our problem is to see what can be said for that principle.

We come closer when we consider a second kind of derivation, the kind that has to do with the poem as a finished public product, an "art object," the formal commodity for which you pay your good money. Regardless of where the poem started, of how many revisions he made, of what he added or left out, etc., etc., here is a self-consistent symbol-system, a structure with beginning, middle, and end, a whole with internally related parts. And the critic's job is to *appreciate* this production.

The problem of derivation here primarily involves a close step-by-step analysis of the particular text, with the attempt to show how the various elements in the work require one another in the course of shaping and guiding and exploiting the expectations of the reader.

Quite as I would not sacrifice the high-class gossip of genetic criticism, so I would be all the more loath to abandon this realm of formal and appreciative criticism, ranging from mere "news" of a work (as in a book review) to such concerns with the principles of a literary species as are embodied in Aristotle's treatise on Greek Tragedy.

But this reference to "the principles of a literary species" brings us to the crux of these notes, which concerns the following paradox: Once you begin asking about the principles involved in the production of a given work, you set the conditions for a surprising kind of reversal. Strictly speaking, it is not the same kind of reversal as we mentioned with regard to the way in which a Poe "story of ratiocination" might be planned by beginning at the end. But the two methods are sufficiently alike to become confused, unless there is a specific attempt to draw the distinction and maintain it. My job here is first to make the distinction clear, and then to show, on the basis of it, how significant Poe's essay becomes, as a guide for critics.

There is a third kind of "derivation," thus:

The critic, let us say, begins with the work as "art object" or "formal commodity," the finished public product. In examining it, he sees that a great many principles of judgment are implicit in it. That is, regardless of whether the author of the work explicitly asked himself why he formed the work as he did, the work embodies a series of decisions which *imply* answers to such questions. For instance, if the work is a play with a blood-and-thunder ending, implicit in its sheer nature there is, first of all, a principle that amounts to saying: "Resolved: That this kind of work should be a play with a blood-and-thunder ending." Similarly, if the author adopts certain procedures for leading to this ending, implicit in these procedures there are principles that amount to saying: "Resolved: That such-and-such kinds of characters in such-and-such kinds of situations and undergoing such-and-such transformations are the proper procedures for a work of this sort." Etc. In brief, insofar as a work is developed in accordance with the author's sense of propriety (insofar as he constructs it in ways that "feel right" to him), then no matter how spontaneous and purely "intuitive" his approach to his material may be, implied in all his choices there is a corresponding set of "principles." However, in his capacity purely as the writer of the original work, he need never state these principles.

As a matter of fact, usually authors do aim to state some of the principles by which they are guided, or think themselves guided. That is, they'll make fragmentary approaches to such "statements of policy" as are to be found grandly in Sidney's *Apologie for Poetrie,* or Wordsworth's preface to the *Lyrical Ballads,* or Shelley's *Defence of Poetry.* But usually their pronouncements along these lines are much less thorough-going than that, being confined to rules of thumb (as with notions that the kind of work they want should be statuesque rather than conversational, or conversational rather than statuesque, or should avoid rhyme, or should never be without rhyme, or should avoid inversions, etc.).

But for our present purposes, the point to be stressed is: Whether or not authors do formulate the principles of choice by which they are guided, such principles are necessarily implicit in the choices they make. Indeed, only by such an internal consistency of principles can the work itself possess the consistency needed to give it integrity and development as an artistic form.

Even if the poet does formulate such principles, however, he does so not as a poet but as another self, as critic. For it is the *critic's* job to attempt systematically specifying the principles of composition that he finds (or thinks he finds) embodied in the given poem. And insofar as the poet himself makes such pronouncements, about either his own work or other people's (as for instance in the prefaces of Racine), he is here speaking as a critic. Often, on this score, he does a much better job of it than the critics themselves—but the fact remains that, at these times, he is writing not poetry but criticism. And whether or not the poet wants to concern himself with such matters, he is certainly entitled to *demand* that the critic do so. He is entitled to *demand* that the critic aim at a conceptual architectonic which will somehow contrive to translate the poet's intuitions into the terms of their corresponding critical principles.

But insofar as the critic proves himself equal to this task, the whole issue can now be turned around. For "principles" are "firsts." As such, they were "there from the very start." In the sense of purely *logical* priority, "principles of composition" implicit in a given literary species (such as a lyric like *The Raven*) "were there even *before*" they became embodied in the particular work that exemplifies them. They "were there," I say, in the sense of a purely *logical* priority—but, especially in the history-ridden nineteenth century (and its twentieth-century vestiges), there has been a constant invitation to interpret all such purely *logical* priority in terms of *temporal* priority.

We now have the material for showing the essential rightness of Poe's concern with "the principle" of composition, however badly he got sidetracked in the effort to develop a truly "principled" theory of poetic derivation. He really did ask himself, as a *critic*, what principles he found (or thought he found) implicit in his act as *poet* (author of *The Raven*). In effect, he thus formulated the esthetic principles (including a theory of beauty and of lyrical effects) which seemed to him the conceptual equivalents of the principles that had implicitly guided him in the writing of the poem. So far, so good.

Then he tricked himself into explaining such procedures in terms of a purely "genetic" (narrative, temporal) series, as with the first kind of critical analysis we considered in these notes. And hereby he opened himself to the distrust that his essay has aroused since the day of its publication.

As noted previously, it's possible that, because of his peculiar approach to such matters, he did come much closer to such a way of working than do most writers. But that's not the main point, for our present purposes. The main point is that he hit upon the ideal form for an "architectonic" critic to aim at.

In other words, regardless of how any work arose (as tested by the gossip available to us when narratively studying the genetic process of the poem's emergence in time), the critic should aim to formulate the principles of composition implicit in it. Then he should test the power and scope of his formulations by reversing the process. Thus, "prophesying after the event," he would proceed by showing how, if his formulations are adequate, the poem should be "logically deducible" from the principles he has formulated.

Ironically enough, the poet usually distrusts any such tendencies in critics. But the poet should reverse his attitude on this matter. He should demand that critics prove themselves worthy of poetry by performing an equally creative task of their own. For if the poet can prod the critics to performances of this sort, then criticism will help reveal the essentially *principled* nature of the judgments underlying the production of the original works.

Thus, instead of stopping with the obvious faults in Poe's essay, let's recognize what an admirably sound critical procedure was struggling for expression there. The changes in style of presentation would be surprisingly slight (though they would amount to the kind of deflection at the center that shows up as quite a deflection at the circumference). Essentially, the shift would amount to this:

Poe need simply have said: "Implicit in my composition there are certain principles. Regardless of how I happened to write this composition, it necessarily embodies these principles. As a critic, I have sought to formulate these principles. Then (just as people check multiplication by division, or addition by subtraction) I'll check my critical formulations by reversing things; and instead of driving the critical principles from the examination of the work, I'll try deriving the work from the principles."

Then he might have added: "Insofar as the principles I have formulated do not seem to account for as much as I would have them do, other critics should try their own hand at the same game, to see whether they can formulate the principles *they* think are needed, to account for the nature of the work."

In sum: To write the poem at all, the poet necessarily writes a certain *kind* of poem. Insofar as the poem is effective, it will necessarily produce a certain *kind* of effect. And the poem is necessarily composed of the elements by which it produced the particular kind of effect "proper" to that particular kind of poem.

Turn this situation around, and the particular methods and subject matter of the poem can be, as it were, "deduced" or "derived" from the definition of the poem as a kind. Thus, Poe tried to persuade his readers that he deduced the topic and treatment of *The Raven* not just "in principle" but actually (genetically) from his definition of what he considered to be the ideal lyric.

However, while arguing for Poe's derivations "in principle," I still feel that his particular formulas must be considerably modified, before we shall have the best "principles" for "prophesying after the event" in Poe's case. Possibly, we need more than his definition of what he takes to be the ideal lyric, or any such definition. Possibly, for a complete job of such "derivation in principle," we should also need a formula for Poe's particular personality (at least, his particular personality as a poet, regardless of what he may have been as citizen and tax-payer). Such considerations would also involve the belowthe-beltism to which we referred in connection with Harry Levin's observation.

For instance with regard to Poe's preferences for dead women as a "beautiful" topic for a poem, we might recall that, in *La Vita Nuova,* Dante tells how he dreamed of Beatrice as dead while she was still alive. Whatever the *psychological* motives for such a fantasy, and whether or not in some cases it is "necrophile," there is the purely *logological* fact that death is a species of *perfection* (that is, "finishedness"). And however differently Dante and Poe may have conceived of poetry, both were concerned with *perfection* as a poetic motive.

Many concerns of this sort would need treatment, for a fully rounded discussion of Poe's essay. But though I have a small bbl. of notes on the subject, these would call for another, quite different presentation.

Along these lines, there is a beautifully relevant passage in *The Meaning of Virgil for our World of Today,* by J. W. Mackail. Here the author points up the nature of the *Aeneid* by saying not what the poem *is* but what it *ought to be* (as though the poem were still to be written, in accord with his specifications). Yet he is "putting in an order" for exactly the kind of poem that the *Aeneid* actually is. For instance, to pick a few details that most quickly illustrate the method:

"The work must be a national poem. . . . It must establish and vindicate the vital interconnection of Rome with Italy. . . . It must link up Rome and the new nation to the Greek civilization. . . . It must bring well into the foreground of the picture the historic conflict between Rome and Carthage. . . . It must celebrate the feats of heroes. . . . It must find expression for the romantic spirit, in its two principal fields of love and adventure. . . . It must exalt the new regime, etc."

There are twelve sets of such "specifications." But a still better example is in the second paragraph of Wordsworth's Preface to the second edition of *Lyrical Ballads:*

"The principal object, then, which I proposed to myself in these Poems was to chuse incidents and situations throughout, as far as was possible, in a selection of language really used by men, and, at the same time, to throw over them a certain colouring of imagination, whereby ordinary things should be presented to the mind in an unusual way; and, furthermore, and above all, to make these incidents and situations interesting by tracing in them, truly though not ostentatiously, the primary laws of our nature; chiefly as far as regards the manner in which we associate ideas in a state of excitement."

From *Poetry*, XCIX (October, 1961), pp. 46-53.